6.99   REL

D0531658

Sikhism for Today

...last date shown below.

Kanwaljit Kaur-Singh

OXFORD
UNIVERSITY PRESS

About the series

We live in a world where there are people of many different religions. In many of our towns and cities Buddhists, Christians, and Jews live alongside Muslims, Hindus, and Sikhs. If you travel abroad you will soon experience whole countries that have been shaped by religion.

We all have different ways of looking at things. It could be said that we all see the world through our own "spectacles". These spectacles are made up of our beliefs, opinions, attitudes, and values. What is important to you might not be important to me.

Religious people see the world through their spectacles, and this affects the way they see and live in the world. We can't understand someone else's world view unless we look through their spectacles. The *Religion for Today* series helps you to do this by giving you the skills and knowledge to understand people with beliefs different from your own.

In learning about another religion you will also be given the chance to think about your own life. So you will not only learn *about* the religions you study; you will also learn *from* the religions.

Chris Wright, Series Editor

About this book

Sikhism started in Punjab, India, but now Sikhs live in many countries around the world. This book introduces you to the way of life of Sikhs by looking at their religious practices and celebrations, the teachings of their Gurus, and their ideas about their responsibilities to society.

Sikhism is one of the youngest of the major religions, only about 530 years old. It addresses many issues that concern people today. You will learn that the ideas of Guru Nanak, who founded Sikhism, contrasted with the intolerance of the times in which he lived, and that Guru Tegh Bahadur laid down his life to uphold the rights of Hindu believers. The Gurus' teaching that people should respect the beliefs of others makes Sikhism a leader in inter-faith dialogue.

The Gurus taught that there is one God and that all human beings are equal in God's eyes. They criticised racism. They condemned the idea that women were inferior to men and gave women equal status with men in all areas of life. They taught that everyone must do his or her duty towards society by serving others, and putting the needs of others first.

You will find that, as you learn about Sikhs from reading this book, you will also have many opportunities to reflect on your own principles and ways of behaving.

Kanwaljit Kaur-Singh

Some background information

▶ Sikhs do not allow anyone to act as a Guru. Therefore, if you want to act out some of the stories, use another character in the scene who says: "I can hear the Guru say ..."

▶ A number of paintings of the Sikh Gurus are reproduced in this book. These are copies of artists' impressions that were painted in the early twentieth century. There are no actual portraits or photos of the Gurus, as the Gurus forbade any type of picture or statue worship.

▶ All dates in the book are Common Era (CE).

▶ We know about the lives of the Gurus from their writings, from historians of the times, and from government documents of the day, which are still available to study.

▶ We know about Sikh teachings from the Guru Granth Sahib, which consists of the writings of the Gurus. The Guru Granth Sahib has been translated into many languages.

▶ Words that you may not be familiar with are explained in the text and also in the Glossary at the back of the book.

Contents

Who are Sikhs?

Sikhism started in the fifteenth century in Punjab, a province in the north of India. Punjab is sometimes called the "homeland" of Sikhs as the majority of Sikhs in the world, approximately 14 million, still live there. Punjab means "the land of five rivers". (In the Panjabi language "punj" is five and "ab" is water.) Most of the Sikhs in Punjab are farmers and they have a reputation for being hard workers. Punjab is known as the bread-basket of India.

Although the majority of Sikhs live in India, many have settled in other countries including Malaysia, Singapore, East Africa, Britain, Australia, New Zealand, Canada, and the USA. There are about 400,000 Sikhs in Britain.

"Sikh" means a disciple, "one who is learning about God". The word is used for all people who follow the Sikh religion.

"Guru" means a teacher. Sikhs believe in the teachings of the founder of the religion, Guru Nanak, his nine successors, and the Guru Granth Sahib, the Sikh holy book. Sikhs do not use the word "Guru" for any other human being. They believe that the Gurus were especially important people who gave God's teachings to their fellow human beings. The Gurus taught that there is only one God, who has made the universe and is present in everything. All people are God's children and should be treated equally.

1 Before you start to study this book, write down in a few sentences what you know about Sikhs. Keep what you write, to look at later.

The province of Punjab was split in 1947 between India and Pakistan. Some sixty per cent of the Sikhs in India live in Punjab.

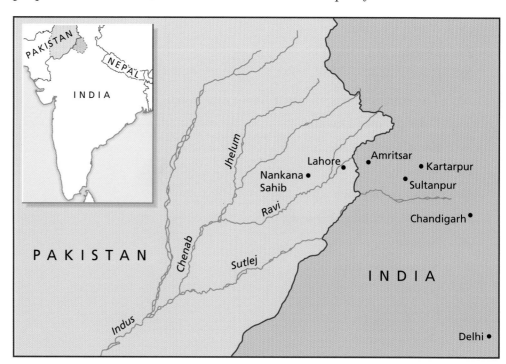

Sikhs at an international conference. Most Sikh women wear Punjabi suits, which consist of kameez (a dress), salwar (a pair of trousers), and dupatta (a scarf). Sikh men generally wear a turban. Sometimes they wear the traditional kurta (a long, loose shirt) and jodhpur-style trousers, but mostly they dress in Western-style clothes.

Mr Ranjit Singh joined Bolingbroke Secondary School to teach mathematics.

Year 7 pupils asked him, "Sir, why do you wear a turban?"

Mr Singh replied, "I am a Sikh. A turban is part of the uniform of my faith. I do not cut my hair but tie it on top of my head and cover it with the turban. My son, who has not yet learned to tie a turban, covers his hair with a large handkerchief called a patka."

"What about your wife and daughter?" Janet asked. "Do they cut their hair?" "No," Mr Singh replied. "Sikh men and women keep their hair un-cut. My wife wears her un-cut hair tied neatly in a bun at the back of her head. My daughter wears her hair loose or plaited."

Mr Singh continued to explain that Sikhs wear "Five Ks":

kes – un-cut hair. It is a sign of saintliness.

kanga – a comb, to keep the hair neat. It represents cleanliness.

kachh – a pair of shorts. It is a symbol of the Sikhs' vow of sexual purity and self-control.

kara – a steel bangle. It is a symbol which reminds Sikhs to do right.

kirpan – a sword. This is a symbol to remind Sikhs to defend the weak.

"Wearing the Five Ks reminds Sikhs that they are all expected to live their lives according to the Gurus' teachings," said Mr Singh. "You could compare the Five Ks to the uniform of, for instance, a policeman, or a priest, or your own school uniform."

2 *Many people emigrate from their homeland and settle in another country in another part of the world. What examples can you think of? Many Sikhs have left India and settled in other countries. What different reasons do people have for leaving their country of origin?*

3 *Do you think that Sikhs wearing their turbans are likely to meet more prejudice in schools and work places than other non-white people?*

4 *What do the words "Guru" and "Sikh" mean? What do you have to believe in to be called a Sikh?*

two

The Basis of Sikhism

Sikhism was started by Guru Nanak in the fifteenth century. In this unit you will learn why there was a need for a new religion at that time and what the Sikh religion grew from. You will hear some Sikhs talking about the religion's emphasis on equality.

During the time of Guru Nanak (1469-1539), Hindus and Muslims were the two major religious communities in India. There was fighting between them as each tried to show that its religion was better than the other's. There was little social contact between Hindus and Muslims. To make matters worse, the Mughal rulers, who were Muslims, were forcing Hindus to convert to Islam, the religion of Muslims.

The majority of people were Hindus and their community was guided by Brahmins, the Hindu priestly class. However, the Brahmins had become selfish and were explaining the religion to suit themselves. Ordinary people were not allowed to read the scriptures and, in many cases, had to give large amounts of money to the Brahmins to perform religious ceremonies.

Guru Nanak, who came from a Hindu family, rejected the idea that one religion was better than another. He was against forced conversion. He thought that it was important to tell people that all human beings are the children of the same God and that they should all respect each other's religions. He started Sikhism to teach this important message.

The Mughal rulers did not like this new religion of tolerance and equality and, as a result, two of the Gurus who succeeded Guru Nanak were tortured to death. Sikhs took up arms and defended themselves and the Hindu community against the Mughals. This experience led the Sikhs to become good soldiers.

Later, during the period of British rule in India (1858-1947), the British respected Sikhs for their bravery and employed them in the British army. Sikhs fought with the British in the First and Second World Wars.

One of the key teachings of Guru Nanak, the founder of Sikhism, was that all people should respect each other's different religions. Today, this idea has become more widespread. For example, representatives of different faiths meet together to discuss environmental issues. Here, the Sikh banner leads the way at the opening ceremony of a conference on the environment.

1 If your country were ruled by a foreign power, and the rulers forced you to accept their religion, would you give up your own faith or would you resist? Why? If you chose to resist, what action would you take?

Some young Sikhs were asked why it was important to them to be a Sikh and why they thought people should know about their religion. These are some of their answers:

66 Sikhism is now well established in Britain as a major world religion. There are over 300 gurdwaras (places of worship) and over 400,000 Sikhs living here. We need to understand our religion and explain it to others so that we can remove prejudices and live in peace with others. 99
[Rema]

66 Sikhism teaches tolerance and respect for other religions. I find this very important. I do not say to other people that my religion is the only true religion and others are all false. This helps me to get on with others with respect. 99
[Satwant]

66 I like the equality given to women in the Sikh religion. I enjoy conducting religious services and ceremonies in the gurdwara equally with my brother. 99
[Charan]

66 Sikhism teaches me to work hard, whether it is to study or to do a job. Then I am to serve others with whatever I have. This sharing of talents or money reminds me of my duties to others and helps me not to be selfish. 99
[Simran]

66 Sikhism teaches me that all people are equal. A person's colour, gender, religion or social status does not matter. It is how we behave that is important. It helps me to respect others and in return be respected by others. 99
[Pam]

Before they start to wear a turban, Sikh boys wear a rumal (a head-covering which is simpler to manage).

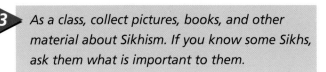

2 ▶ *Look at the young Sikhs' statements about the importance of Sikhism. Which ones appeal to you most? Compare your choices with those of a friend and discuss why you liked the statements you chose.*

3 ▶ *As a class, collect pictures, books, and other material about Sikhism. If you know some Sikhs, ask them what is important to them.*

Sikh soldiers.

Guru Nanak's Childhood

Guru Nanak, the founder of Sikhism, was born in 1469 in Talwandi – later called Nankana Sahib – now in Pakistan. Nanak's father, Kalu, worked as an accountant and owned considerable land. He was a high-caste Hindu, and was proud of this and of his riches.

Nanak was therefore brought up as a high-caste Hindu. At the age of seven he was sent to school, where he was taught Sanskrit, Persian, and Arabic. But Nanak was more interested in learning about God, and liked to talk with and listen to Hindu holy men. Everyone in the village believed that Nanak had special powers given by God.

When Nanak was nine, his family prepared for him to receive the "sacred thread" in a special Hindu ceremony. The ceremony was only for boys born in a high caste. Nanak asked the priest, "Why are you putting the thread round me?" The priest replied that, "Without wearing this thread you will not go to heaven. Only by wearing this will you become a good person." Nanak refused to accept it and said, "Anyone can wear this thread. Besides, it could break, get dirty, get lost, or get burned. I think it is important to speak the truth, be good and kind, and treat all people with respect. Only these good qualities can make a person better and fit to go to heaven." Nanak's father, Kalu, was furious at this. But Nanak was unhappy about religious practices and rituals, particularly those that conveyed the idea that some people were superior to others.

1 ▶ From what you know about Guru Nanak, why do you think he refused to wear the sacred thread?
Do you know of any other person from a rich family who showed that living a good life is more important than wealth or social status?

One day, while working as a cattle grazer, the young Nanak fell asleep in the hot sun. A deadly cobra appeared and shaded him with its hood. A passer-by was horrified at first to see the cobra raise its head as if to strike Nanak, but then realised that the cobra was protecting the boy from the sun's heat.

As a young boy, Nanak kept his mother, Tripta, busy cooking. He used to bring home holy men and poor and hungry people and ask her to feed them.

Tripta knew that Nanak was not an ordinary child, but had special powers from God which ordinary people could not understand.

Guru Nanak's mother Tripta feeds the hungry.

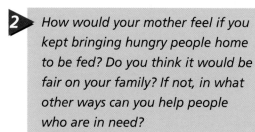

How would your mother feel if you kept bringing hungry people home to be fed? Do you think it would be fair on your family? If not, in what other ways can you help people who are in need?

Why do you think Nanak's father was angry with him? Have you ever done something that made your parents angry? If so, were they right to be angry with you? Do you think you should always agree with your parents? Do your parents expect you always to agree with them?

Nanak's father, Kalu, wanted him to become a rich businessman. He gave Nanak twenty rupees to buy groceries for his shop to sell at a profit. He told him to spend the money wisely (to make a true bargain). On his way to the market, Nanak met a group of holy men who, he discovered, had not eaten anything for a few days and had no money to buy food. Nanak went to the market, bargained hard to get as much food as he could, and returned to give all the food to the hungry men. Kalu was furious. "I told you to spend the money wisely (make a true bargain)," he shouted, and he started beating Nanak. "I did! I fed the poor people. Surely, there is no better bargain than feeding the poor," Nanak replied.

Divine Revelation

1 *Do you have friends who believe in a different religion from yours?*
Do your parents or other friends agree with your friendship?
Do you have friends that your parents don't approve of?
Imagine how you would feel if your parents asked you to stop a particular friendship. Write a few sentences arguing why you should continue the friendship.

In Guru Nanak's time, Indian society was torn apart by fighting between Hindus and Muslims. The majority of the population was Hindu but the Mughals, who had conquered India, were Muslims. They were determined to convert the whole of the Indian population to their religion.

From an early age Nanak was friendly with both Mardana, a Muslim, and Bala, a Hindu. His friendship with Mardana was frowned upon by everyone, particularly his father, for generally Hindus and Muslims did not mix in this way. But Nanak refused to give up his friendship with Mardana and it lasted until Mardana died of old age.

Every day, Nanak went to the river to bathe. One day a passer-by noticed Nanak bathing, but looked again a moment later and realised that he had disappeared. The passer-by looked and looked for Nanak, but could not find him. Other people came to search. They saw Nanak's clothes on the river bank, but there was no other sign of him. A servant of the Chief of Sultanpur ran to tell his master of Nanak's disappearance.

"Send all the divers to look for Nanak. He is my most trustworthy and honest officer. I am lost without him," the Chief told his servant. "And you might as well ask the fishermen to cast their nets in the river in search of him. Find him, find him." But they could not find Nanak.

Nanak was missing for three days. Everyone thought that he had drowned, and had given up hope of finding even his body when Nanak suddenly turned up at his family home. He did not say a single word for two days, but on the third day he spoke: "There is neither a Hindu nor a Muslim, but only man." Everyone was puzzled. They knew that there were Hindus and Muslims living in Sultanpur. They asked Nanak to explain the mystery behind his words.

"I had a vision of God, and now I must preach God's message," he said. "God is the creator of all, and loves everyone. We all are God's

2 *How would you feel if a member of your family or a friend disappeared for a few days?*
How would you celebrate if he/she came back alive and well?

3 *Write a short letter to your friend who has missed some lessons due to illness. Explain what Nanak experienced during his revelation.*

children. Hindus and Muslims should live as brothers and sisters, as one family of God." The townspeople and the holy men who were Nanak's companions realised that Nanak was a changed person. He was now giving them a message from God and they started calling him "Guru".

Guru Nanak left his job with the Chief of Sultanpur, saying: "I am going to serve God and God alone." He gave all his personal belongings to the poor and needy, and set out with Mardana to preach God's message.

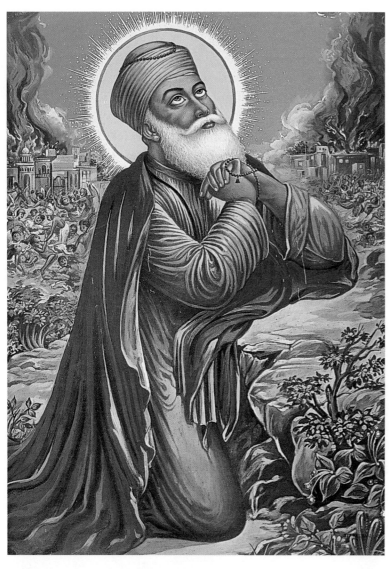

In this representation of Guru Nanak's revelation, the artist has shown fighting and destruction in the background. Guru Nanak understood that such fighting between Hindus and Muslims made no sense, since all people were children of the same one God.

4 ▶ Have you had any experience which has made you think differently or see things in a new light?
What pictures would you draw to show how people can start to look at things in a new way?

66 I was a minstrel out of work
   Called to divine service.
Night and day I sing His praise.
The Master summoned the minstrel
To the high court
And robed me with the clothes of honour. 99
[Guru Granth Sahib, page 150]

Guru Nanak's Teaching on Helping Others

Guru Nanak made four missionary journeys: east as far as Assam, in India, south to Sri Lanka, north to Tashkent, and west to Mecca in Saudi Arabia.

On one of his journeys the Guru was invited for a meal at the home of Duni Chand, a rich banker who had hoarded a great deal of money. Every time he made a million rupees, he would put a flag outside his house. He had many flags flying, but never thought of helping the poor. When the Guru was leaving, Duni Chand asked if he could be of any service to him. He was hoping that the Guru would bless him with more riches, so that he would be able to put more flags outside his house to impress others with his wealth. But the Guru gave Duni Chand a needle and asked him to return it to him in the next world. Duni Chand asked how he could take the needle to the next world, to which Guru Nanak replied, "In the same way as you will take your riches." This made Duni Chand feel ashamed of his greed and miserliness and, from that day, he used his wealth to help the poor. The Guru's message was that helping the poor is also a way of serving God.

 1 *Do you agree that helping others is a way of serving God? Explain your views.*

The Guru writes:

66 Accursed is the life which is lived only to fatten oneself. 99

[Guru Granth Sahib, page 790]

 2 *Write a paragraph about the message given by Guru Nanak in the story of Duni Chand. Do you know any real or television character who had a similar attitude to hoarding wealth and then changed his/her views and started to help the poor? Write a paragraph about the result of that change.*

Guru Nanak's four missionary journeys.

Map legend:
- 1500–1505
- 1506–1509
- 1514–1516
- 1518–1521

Guru Nanak wanted people to take helping others as an important responsibility, since he believed that all human beings are God's children. Once during his travels, he and Mardana stopped outside a village, tired and hungry. The Guru sat down and Mardana went into the village. But the villagers were inhospitable, rude, and violent. Mardana came away empty-handed. The Guru got up and said a prayer asking God to bless the villagers that they should remain happy and contented in this village.

The Guru and Mardana walked on and, outside the next village, the Guru again sat down and sent Mardana to ask for food and shelter. The villagers welcomed him and invited the two men to stay. After a few days, the Guru and Mardana thanked the villagers for their hospitality and went on their way. Just outside the village, the Guru stopped and said a prayer asking God to bless the villagers and scatter them far and wide.

Mardana was astonished. He asked, "Why bless the inhospitable people in the first village and pray that the people who have shown us hospitality should lose their homes and move on to new places? This seems to be a curse and not a blessing." "No," the Guru replied. "Wherever the hospitable villagers go they will take their goodness with them and will teach their noble habits to others. That is why I want them to move. It will be better for the human race if the selfish people of the first village remain settled so that they do not share their bad qualities with others."

3 ▶ *The Guru gave his message through stories. Do you think that people understand a message better through stories?*

4 ▶ *Do you agree with the views expressed in the story of the two villages? Explain your opinion. Think about friends or relatives who have been helpful to you. What sort of help have they given you?*

SIX

Guru Nanak's Teaching on How To Worship God

In this unit you will learn how Guru Nanak taught people to think more about the message contained in their religion, and not to follow rituals without remembering their meaning.

Guru Nanak taught that praying involves more than just saying the words of a prayer; it means acting according to the truth contained in the prayer. Once a Nawab (the head of a small principality) and a Qazi (a Muslim priest) said to the Guru: "You say that Hindus and Muslims are all children of the same God. We all pray to the same and only God. If that is true, then why not come and pray in the mosque with us?" The Guru readily agreed.

When the Qazi stood up to pray, everyone stood and joined him except the Guru, who remained seated. Afterwards the Nawab asked why he had not joined in. The Guru said that he had wanted to join in the prayer as he had promised, but that neither the Qazi nor the Nawab had been present. They argued that everyone knew that they had been there and had been praying.

"But where were your minds?" asked the Guru. He then suggested quite accurately that the Nawab had been thinking about buying horses in a market in Kabul. The Qazi asked, "But what about joining me? I was praying." The Guru replied that the Qazi had been worrying about his newly born foal, who was not tied securely. The two men realised that they had just been saying the prayer without thinking about its meaning.

1 What lessons do you learn from the story of Guru Nanak, the Nawab, and the Qazi? Do you sometimes have difficulty in concentrating on what you are doing? What can you do to help you concentrate better?

14

When Guru Nanak visited Mecca, he was tired from travelling and fell asleep near the Ka'bah, the cube-shaped holy building of Islam, which Muslims´ face towards when they pray. A Qazi, who had come to say evening prayers, saw that the Guru's feet were pointing towards the Ka'bah and told the Guru off: "Why are you pointing your feet towards the house of God?" The Guru replied, "Turn my feet to the direction where there is no house of God." The Qazi dragged the Guru's feet round but, whichever position he moved them to, the Ka'bah also moved. The Qazi realised that God is everywhere.

The Guru writes:

66 Rituals and ceremonies can be the chains of the mind 99

and also:

66 Cursed be the ritual that makes us forget God. 99

[Guru Granth Sahib, pages 635 and 590]

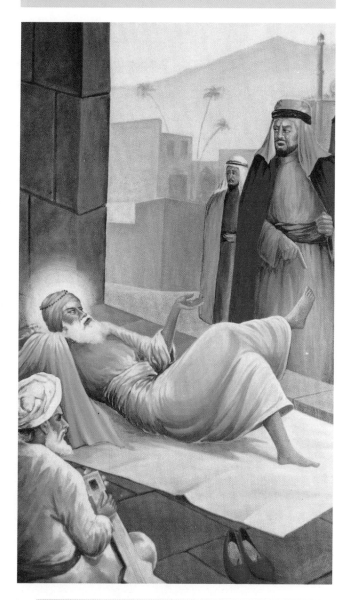

The Qazi reproaches Guru Nanak who has fallen asleep with his feet pointing towards the Ka'bah.

Guru Nanak taught that, although rituals can sometimes be useful in concentrating the mind, following rituals blindly, without remembering their meaning, does more harm than good. Rituals can distract people from the real purpose of religion. At Hardwar, he saw people standing in the river and throwing water eastwards towards the rising sun. On enquiring why, he was told that they were giving water to their dead ancestors. The Guru started to throw water in the opposite direction, which made the people laugh and ask, "Why are you throwing water towards the west?" The Guru replied, "I am watering my fields in Punjab. If your water can reach millions of miles away to your ancestors, then my water can certainly reach my fields which are only some hundreds of miles from here."

▶ Left: Guru Nanak copies people throwing water at Hardwar, except that he throws it in the opposite direction from them. What was he trying to teach them? In what ways do you think they might have reacted?

2 ▶ Why did Guru Nanak throw water in the opposite direction from the other people? Make a poster illustrating the story and choose a title which explains the message the Guru tried to give.

SEVEN

The Second and Third Gurus

Guru Nanak started a succession of Gurus, who continued to teach by example and to develop the new faith. In this unit you will learn about the second and third Gurus, and think about the qualities that you respect in people.

Guru Nanak chose Guru Angad Dev to be the Guru after him, and each Guru then chose his own successor. There were ten human Gurus.

Guru Nanak believed that the person he chose to lead the young Sikh community needed to be humble, dedicated to the cause, and willing to serve others. Legend says that Guru Nanak set a test to see who would be the right person for the Guruship. He deliberately dropped a cup into a muddy ditch and asked his two sons to fetch it for him. They refused to go in the muddy water and dirty their clothes, and asked why the Guru had dropped the cup in the first place. By contrast, Angad jumped into the water and fetched the cup, showing his dedication to the Guru.

1 *What qualities of Guru Angad made him worthy to be the Guru after Guru Nanak? Would you like your friends to have these qualities?*

Guru Angad Dev

Guru Angad Dev became the second Guru in 1539 and died in 1552. He is remembered especially for improving the Gurmukhi script for writing Panjabi. Panjabi was the everyday language spoken in Punjab, but at the time of Guru Nanak there was no agreed form of writing it.

Gurmukhi means "from the mouth of the Guru" and it is the alphabet in which all the Sikh scriptures are written. Guru Angad made a collection of Guru Nanak's shabads (hymns) and wrote down his own so that ordinary people could read them.

Guru Angad Dev teaches some Sikhs the Gurmukhi script.

Guru Amar Das

Guru Amar Das became the third Guru in 1552 and died in 1574. He stressed the equality of women with men, introduced women preachers, and started fifty-two study circles to give education to women.

Indian society was divided by the caste system. Families belonged to a particular caste (or section of society), often depending on their occupation. Some castes were thought "higher" than others, and people from "lower" castes were treated badly. Marriages between people from different castes were forbidden.

Guru Amar Das opposed the caste system by encouraging everyone to sit and eat together as one family of God. The practice of eating together after every Sikh service (known as "langar") has continued ever since. When the Mughal emperor Akbar came to meet Guru Amar Das, he too was required to sit and eat with ordinary people.

Another tradition started by Guru Amar Das was for all Sikhs who could do so to gather in his home town on the festivals of Diwali and Baisakhi. This meant that the Guru could meet his followers personally.

Emperor Akbar and his officers sit and eat langar with Guru Amar Das and other Sikhs.

Eating langar today, after a service at a gurdwara in Patna, India. All gurdwara services are followed by langar. (See Unit Sixteen.)

2 *List the actions Guru Amar Das took to ensure that all people were treated equally.*

Guru Angad's son, Dattu, forgot that the Guruship was awarded on merit and thought that it was his right to become the Guru after his father. When he saw Guru Amar Das sitting in his father's place, he kicked him. Guru Amar Das caught hold of Dattu's foot and began massaging it. He explained, "I am massaging you just in case my old bones have hurt your tender foot."

Guru Amar Das taught forgiveness:

66 Those who hit you do not hit them back.
But go to their homes and kiss their feet,
Asking for forgiveness for causing any pain. 99
[Guru Granth Sahib, page 1378]

EIGHT

The Fourth, Fifth, and Sixth Gurus

Guru Ram Das, the fourth Guru

Guru Ram Das became the fourth Guru in 1574 and died in 1581. He founded the city of Amritsar and encouraged Sikh traders and business people to settle there. Sikhs also gathered in Amritsar for the festivals of Baisakhi and Diwali. So the new city soon grew into a large trading and religious centre.

The Guru continued to preach against social customs that gave women an inferior status. He encouraged widows to remarry. He also composed a wedding hymn called "Lavan", which is read and sung at every Sikh wedding service.

Guru Ram Das carries bricks for the building of Amritsar.

A view of Amritsar today.

1 *What were Guru Arjan's two great contributions to the Sikh community?*

2 *Why did Guru Hargobind wear two swords and encourage his Sikhs to train in warfare?*

3 *Why is it important for the teachings of a religion to be written down?*

Guru Arjan, the fifth Guru

Guru Ram Das chose his son to become the Guru after him. Guru Arjan continued the building of Amritsar which his father had started and built a beautiful gurdwara there, in the middle of an artificial lake. This gurdwara is the Harimandir Sahib, now more commonly known as the Golden Temple. The building was designed to have four doors, to show that it was open to all people. The Guru wrote:

> "The four castes of Kashatria, Brahman, Sudras and Vaisyas
> Are equal partners in divine instruction."
> (Guru Granth Sahib, page 747)

Guru Arjan compiled the Adi Granth, which is now known as the Guru Granth Sahib (the Sikh holy book). He collected the hymns of the first four Gurus and added his own. The work was completed in 1604, and was installed in the Golden Temple.

The Mughal emperor Jehangir could not tolerate the Guru's popularity and tried to force him to become a Muslim and also to make changes in the Guru Granth Sahib. When the Guru refused, he was tortured to death in 1606. (See Unit Twenty-two.)

A "granthi" reads the Guru Granth Sahib in the Golden Temple.

Guru Hargobind, the sixth Guru

Guru Arjan Dev's eleven-year-old son, Hargobind, became Guru in 1606, on his father's death. He realised the need for non-Muslim people to defend their faiths. He organised the Sikh community to defend the weak and helpless. He wore two swords, one symbolising the spiritual power of God's truth and the other showing his readiness to use actual physical strength to defend others. (See Unit Twenty-three.)

Guru Arjan writes:

66 However handsome, well-born, wise,
Clever in speech and wealthy,
He is no more than a corpse,
If the love of God is not in his heart. 99

 4 *The Muslim rulers tried to force Guru Arjan to become a Muslim and to make changes to the Guru Granth Sahib. The Guru believed that everyone has a right to choose his/her own religion. When he refused to do what the government wanted, he was put to death without any trial. Compare the government's actions with those of a bully. What can people do if a government acts like a bully? What would you have done if you had been a Sikh in the time of Guru Arjan Dev and Guru Hargobind?*

The two swords of Guru Hargobind form part of the Sikh "khanda" symbol. The symbol also includes a double-edged sword, standing for God's power as creator, and a circle, standing for continuity.

nine

The Last Four Gurus

In this unit you will learn about the seventh, eighth, ninth, and tenth Gurus. You will see how Guru Gobind Singh ended the line of human Gurus by passing the Guruship to the Guru Granth Sahib.

Guru Har Rai and Guru Har Krishan

Guru Har Rai was the seventh Guru, from 1644 to 1661, and Guru Har Krishan was the eighth Guru, from 1661 to 1664. This was a fairly quiet period, during which the Gurus helped to provide free medical aid to the needy. Guru Har Krishan died at the age of eight, from smallpox contracted while he was serving the sick.

Guru Har Krishan, the eighth Guru, in the dispensary.

Guru Tegh Bahadur, the ninth Guru

Guru Tegh Bahadur was Guru from 1664 to 1675, during which time the Mughal emperor Aurengzeb was forcing Hindus in his empire to convert to Islam. Anyone who refused was killed. The Hindu Brahmins appealed to Guru Tegh Bahadur to save them from the emperor's persecution. Though not a Hindu, the Guru offered to help the Brahmins as he believed in the basic human right of people to practise their own religion. He spoke to the emperor on the Brahmins' behalf and this led to his imprisonment and execution. (See Unit Twenty-two.)

> 66 To uphold righteousness, so supreme an act did he perform;
>   He gave his head, but did not utter a word of sorrow.
> For the sake of righteousness he did this heroic deed;
> He laid down his life but not the principles.
> No one has done such a unique deed as Guru Tegh Bahadur. 99
> *[Guru Gobind Singh]*

Guru Gobind Singh, the tenth Guru

Guru Gobind Singh was Guru from 1675 to 1708, during which time Sikhs were being killed by the Mughal rulers. The Guru had to fight many battles to defend his young Sikh community against the Mughal armies, who were far superior in numbers and equipment. His two older sons died in battle and the younger two were walled up alive for refusing to accept Islam.

The Guru organised the Sikhs so that they would be able to defend the weak and their own community. He wanted his Sikhs to be so brave that, even in moments of weakness, they would not deny their faith. On the festival of Baisakhi in 1699, he tested the Sikhs to see if they were ready to defend their faith, even at the risk of their lives. When they passed that test (see page 49), the Guru asked them to wear the Five Ks as their uniform. The uniform would identify them and remind them of their belief in one God, the equality of all humans, and the importance of showing respect and tolerance towards all.

Guru Gobind Singh then said that, in future, Sikhs should follow the teachings in the Guru Granth Sahib as their Guru. He ended the line of human Gurus.

1 In Britain today, what means are there for Sikhs and others to speak out against any injustice they might meet?

2 Have you or has anyone you know had to fight to get justice in your day-to-day school life? Can you write what the injustice was and how it was sorted out?

3 With a partner, discuss the circumstances in which someone might deny that he or she belongs to a particular group or faith. Can you think of examples from history or from the stories of other religions of people who have denied their faith?

Guru Tegh Bahadur (top left), his son Guru Gobind Singh, and Guru Gobind Singh's four sons. The bricks are a reference to the two younger boys being walled up alive for refusing to give up Sikhism.

ten

Maharajah Ranjit Singh

Mughal rule in India eventually weakened and there was a period of equality and tolerance, under Maharajah Ranjit Singh. Then, during the British Raj (1858-1947), the Sikhs had to stand up for the right to run their own gurdwaras. In this unit you will consider ways of standing up for one's rights.

Sikhs were tortured and killed during the reigns of successive Mughal emperors. Some emperors offered rewards to anyone who could bring them a Sikh dead or alive. There were mass killings of men, women, and children. As Sikhs wore the Five Ks, they were easily recognised. They left their homes and hid in the jungle for safety, refusing to give up their faith. The period from 1708 to 1739 saw the worst suffering in Sikh history. Sikhs did not give up hope but grouped together and, when possible, started guerrilla warfare to defend themselves.

Internal fighting and foreign invasions from the north-west caused the Mughal empire to disintegrate. Often Sikhs fought and defeated the invaders, and eventually they set up their own independent states in Punjab. Twelve of these states became powerful and were known as "Misals".

The ruler of one of the states was Maharajah Ranjit Singh and he soon took control of Punjab and much of India. He was crowned emperor in 1799 and ruled for forty years, treating people of all religions equally. Muslims, Hindus, and Sikhs held important posts in his empire.

The Maharajah gave strict instructions that all people, rich and poor, should be treated fairly. Many stories tell how the Maharajah punished his own close friends and relatives in his determination to ensure that everyone was treated justly and that people of higher status did not receive unfair advantages.

Maharajah Ranjit Singh.

1 *In the story on page 23, why did Hindus and Sikhs complain about the Muslim call to prayer? Why do you think they agreed with the Maharajah's solution?*

The Maharajah died in 1839 and within ten years internal feuding had caused the collapse of the Sikh empire. The British were already ruling the greater part of India and soon conquered Punjab.

The British rulers respected the Sikhs for their bravery and encouraged them to join the British army. However the Sikhs became unhappy with the British Raj (rule) as the British allowed the Sikh historic gurdwaras to fall into the hands of non-Sikhs —

mostly Hindus, who did not let low-caste people enter the gurdwara and did not permit women to conduct services. To win the right to manage their gurdwaras, the Sikhs started a "peaceful agitation", which lasted for about twenty years. Generally, a group of five or six Sikh protesters would march towards the gurdwara saying prayers. The army would beat them to prevent them from entering the gurdwara, and during later protests the army used to open fire. In 1925, the British government finally gave the Sikhs the right to manage their own gurdwaras.

2 *How did the Sikhs protest against British rule? Do you think it is best to protest in a non-violent way? What happens if a government does not respond to peaceful protests?*

▶ *Demonstrations are one way in which a large number of people can show their point of view about something.*
What other non-violent ways of protesting can you think of? Which do you think are most effective and why?

Maharajah Ranjit Singh was keen that all his subjects should have justice. Once some Muslims complained to him that Hindus and Sikhs in their village were not allowing the mullah to give the "call to prayer", which reminds Muslims that it is time for the particular prayers they must say each day. The Maharajah asked the Hindus and Sikhs about this and they told him that the mullah's shrill voice calling from the top of a building five times a day interfered with their work. The Maharajah told the Sikhs and Hindus that, "If you take the responsibility of going around the village

five times a day at the appropriate time informing all Muslims that it is time for prayers, then I will tell these people not to use their shrill voices to do so."

The Hindus and Sikhs replied, "This is an impossible task. How can we run about five times a day to the houses and fields of these people informing them that it is time for prayers?" The Maharajah replied, "Then let the mullah carry on with the call. We must follow our Gurus' teachings and make sure that people of all religions can worship as they want."

ELEVEN

The Sikh Belief in One God

Do you ever think about who or what God is? In this unit you will think about Sikhs' belief in one God and about how they see the relationship between humans and God.

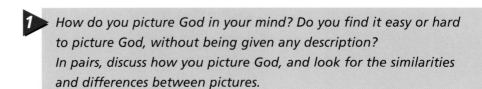

1 How do you picture God in your mind? Do you find it easy or hard to picture God, without being given any description?
In pairs, discuss how you picture God, and look for the similarities and differences between pictures.

Several Sikhs in Britain today were asked about their views of God and gave the answers shown on these two pages.

Sikhs believe that they should always strive to be more God-like and less self-centred. They stress the need to develop their own relationship with God, by seeking truth and leading a good life.

Sikhism rejects ritual and worship that is too formal. Sikhs believe that these put obstacles in the way of developing a direct relationship with God and distract people from the importance of leading a good life.

When they pray, some Sikhs use a "gutka", a book containing extracts from the Guru Granth Sahib. You can find out more about gutkas in Unit Thirteen.

66 The Sikh Gurus taught us that there is only one God. God is described in the opening lines of the Guru Granth Sahib, which I recite every day. These lines, known as the 'Mool Mantra', are:

There is but one God
Whose name is Truth
God the creator is without fear, without hate, immortal
Without form and is beyond birth and death
And is understood through God's grace.

I also have a poster of Ik Onkar which means 'there is one God'. This poster reminds me about God. 99

[Pavan]

The Ik Onkar symbol. It means "one God" and is the first symbol of the "Mool Mantra" in the Gurmukhi script.

> ❝ The Sikh Gurus taught us that God is the creator who has created and is still creating this universe. God has no form or shape and does not take birth and therefore does not die. God is neither male nor female. God is present everywhere at the same time; therefore God cannot be like a human being. If it was so, then God would have millions and millions of eyes, hands, and feet which could be seen. But we cannot see God, because God is more like a spirit that is everywhere in the universe. The human soul is a spark of that spirit. The ultimate aim of each soul is to reach perfection, and become united with God and avoid rebirth in the world. ❞
>
> [Satwant Kaur]

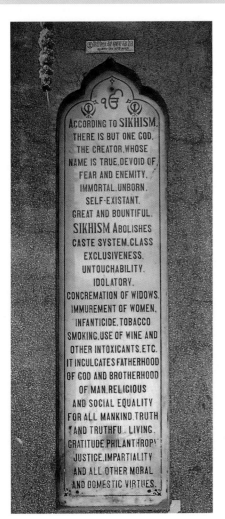

Words outside a gurdwara in Calcutta.

 2 Write a few sentences describing the Sikh view of God.

> ❝ The Sikh Gurus used Hindu names when talking to Hindus about God, and 'Allah' when talking to Muslims, but they always had the Sikh concept of God in their minds. We use many names for God such as 'Akal Purukh' (the Timeless One), 'Karta Purukh' (the Creator), and 'Waheguru' (the Wonderful Lord). I mostly say 'Waheguru'. ❞
>
> [Ranjit Kaur]

> ❝ Sikhs believe that God is the highest authority and that God's truth was given to humanity through the Sikh Gurus and is contained in the Guru Granth Sahib... One can understand God by acting upon the Gurus' teachings. God's acceptance of the sincerity of our actions is called His Grace. ❞
>
> [Indarjit Singh]

> ❝ My religion teaches me that God loves everyone equally and our colour, gender, religious beliefs, or social status do not help or hinder in finding God. It is how we behave towards others that matters. ❞
>
> [Simran Singh]

3 Do you know another religion that believes in only one God? Are there other similarities between that religion and Sikhism?

4 What ways would you suggest to get closer to God?

The Oneness of Humanity

Sikhs believe that God the creator has made one humanity, and so all humans are equal. No one is high or low by birth, and it is the actions of people that make them good or evil.

In Sikhism, men and women are equal and play equal roles in leading services and conducting ceremonies. Sikhs also reject the idea of race. Guru Gobind Singh writes in one of his hymns:

"Recognise there is but one race of all human beings."

Sikh institutions are run according to this idea of equality. Anyone can join and be part of the Sikh sangat (congregation). Gurdwaras (places of worship) are open to all worshippers, regardless of their class, creed, colour, or gender. Every gurdwara contains a langar (community kitchen) where men and women of all classes and colours prepare and serve food after each service. The whole congregation eats together in the langar after a service, to show the togetherness of the one big family of God.

The Guru Granth Sahib (the Sikh holy book) contains the writings not only of Sikhs but also of Hindus and Muslims whose teachings were similar to those of the Gurus. The foundation stone of the Golden Temple in Amritsar was laid by a Muslim holy man. The Golden Temple has doors on all four sides, to welcome people from all directions. This symbolises the idea that good and holy people can belong to any religion.

Men and women take an equal part in preparing the langar food.

Men and women take part equally in Sikh services. Here they play "tabla" (drums) and harmoniums, to accompany the singing of shabads.

“ My religion teaches me that God loves everyone equally, whatever our colour, gender, religious beliefs, or social status. Every day I recite the following hymn from page 1349 of the Guru Granth Sahib:

> The Lord first created Light.
> From the Lord's play all living creatures came,
> And from the Divine Light the whole
>   creation sprang.
> Why then should we divide human creatures
>   into high and low? ...
> The Lord the Maker hath moulded one
>   mass of clay
> Into vessels of diverse shapes.
> Free from taint are all the vessels of clay
> Since free from taint is the Divine Potter.

This reminds me that I must treat everyone equally as they are all God's children. ”

[Simran Singh]

1 ▶ Do you agree that all human beings should be treated equally? Are they treated equally?

2 ▶ Why do you think it is important for you to be treated equally with others? Have you ever been treated unequally? If so, write a paragraph about why you were treated unequally and how you felt about this.

3 ▶ Would the Sikh Gurus have approved of Simon's behaviour in the story below? Explain this. Re-write the story so that it reflects Sikh teachings about equality.

4 ▶ In a group, discuss the Sikh view on equality and give reasons for agreeing or disagreeing with it.

5 ▶ Do you have friends who belong to a different faith group or who are a different colour from you? Do you treat them as equals? Do they treat you as equals? Write a few sentences expressing your views.

▶ The Sikh hymn quoted by Simran Singh includes the words that God has "moulded one mass of clay into vessels of diverse shapes". What does this image of human creation mean, in your view?

Simon's party

Peter came home crying. His mother asked, "Why are you crying? What has upset you?" In between his sobs Peter blurted out, "Simon will be 10 years old and is having his birthday party on Saturday. He has invited all the children, the whole class except me, to his party." "Why? Did you have an argument?" "No. He says I am black and he does not want any black people to his party." Peter's mother gave him a big hug and said, "Don't get upset. We have already planned to take you out for a picnic anyway." Peter was delighted at the thought of an outing to his favourite place.

The Guru Granth Sahib

Guru Nanak wrote hundreds of shabads (hymns) in praise of God and giving advice on how to live a good life. The second, third, and fourth Gurus likewise wrote many shabads. In 1604, Guru Arjan, the fifth Guru, then collected all the writings of the first four Gurus, and added his own together with the writings of Hindu and Muslim saints whose views were in accord with Sikh teachings, to make the Adi Granth. "Adi" means first, in terms of number and importance, and "Granth" means book.

In 1706, Guru Gobind Singh, the tenth Guru, added the writings of the ninth Guru, Guru Tegh Bahadur, and said that Sikhs should now follow the Adi Granth as their Guru. The Adi Granth became known as the Guru Granth Sahib. "Sahib" is a word used to show respect. Sikhism is the only religion in the world to have the original writings of its founders.

For nearly 200 years, copies of the Guru Granth Sahib were written out carefully by hand, making sure that there were no mistakes. In 1852, the first copy was printed. Sikhs have decided that every copy of the book should be exactly the same, containing 1430 pages, with particular hymns always on the same page number. The Guru Granth Sahib is written in Panjabi and the script used is Gurmukhi.

A page from the Guru Granth Sahib.

Guru Arjan Dev compiling the Guru Granth Sahib. The artist has represented the previous Gurus and the Hindu and Muslim saints whose writings were all included.

The Guru Granth Sahib is found at the centre of all Sikh special occasions. Here, as part of a procession to celebrate Guru Nanak's birthday, it is carried – on cushions and under a canopy as usual – on a special float.

1 ▸ *Is there someone or something to which you give special respect? How do you show that respect? How do the actions you take to show your respect make you feel?*

No one is allowed to print copies of the Guru Granth Sahib except the main Sikh body called the Shiromani Gurdwara Parbandhak Committee in Amritsar, and no words, sentences, or hymns can be added or taken away from the book.

Since the Guru Granth Sahib takes the place of the living Guru among Sikhs, it is treated with a reverence similar to that shown to the human Gurus in their lifetime. As the book contains the writings of the Gurus, it is believed to hold the highest authority and it is found at the centre of Sikh ceremonies, festivals, and daily practices.

Guru Arjan compares the Sikh scripture to a dish of food:

> 66 In the plate are placed three things, truth, contentment, and meditation.
> The name of the Lord, the support of all, has also been put therein. Whosoever eats this food will be free from sorrow. 99

[Guru Granth Sahib, page 1429]

2 ▸ *What do you think the girl in the story would have done if the salesman had not given her his gutka? Have there been times when you have not been able to have things that you wanted very badly? How did you feel and what did you do?*

A gutka is a small book containing a collection of hymns and daily prayers from the Guru Granth Sahib. Some people take their gutka to read on the train, to and from work.

My grandmother told me that when she was little (about a hundred years ago), there was only one gutka in her village, from which the teacher taught the children shabads. "I always wanted a gutka of my own," my grandmother remembered. "A salesman came to the village once a month with goods such as soap, sugar, combs, and books, all loaded on to his horse-drawn cart. At the sound of his bell, people would come to the village square. I asked the salesman to get me a gutka and he agreed. Each month I asked him about it, but his reply was always, 'They are out of print.'

"One day I reached the square a little late and, to my horror, saw my cousin buying the only copy of the gutka. I was heart-broken. My mother and father could not console me.

"The next evening the salesman knocked at our door. He said that he could not bear to see me sad and that he had brought me his own copy. I treasured that gutka, until I left it behind when our part of Punjab became Pakistan and we had to leave in a hurry."

FOURTEEN

Showing Respect for the Guru Granth Sahib

How do you show respect in the way that you treat something that is special to you? Do you make sure that your friends treat that item carefully as well? In this unit you will learn how Sikhs show reverence to their holy book, the Guru Granth Sahib.

If you visit a gurdwara you will find the Guru Granth Sahib on a dais, or platform, with a canopy. Resting on cushions and covered with a cloth called romallas, the book is the most prominent feature in the gurdwara. A member of the sangat (congregation) is in constant attendance and waves a chouri (fan) over the Guru Granth Sahib, as a sign of its importance. Overnight, the book is kept in a small room. It is brought out in the morning and installed ceremoniously on the dais. After evening prayers, it is ceremoniously closed and put away again.

When they enter a room where the Guru Granth Sahib is, worshippers must wear no shoes and have their head covered. Before they sit, they bow and touch their forehead against the floor. These are all marks of respect.

Any man or woman may read to the congregation from the Guru Granth Sahib, but quite often the book is read by an appointed granthi who performs ceremonies and conducts prayers.

Waving the chouri over the Guru Granth Sahib is a sign of respect for its importance.

1 *Do you have a special book? Do you look after it better than your other books? What do you like best about this book?*

The whole of the Guru Granth Sahib is written in poetry, arranged in stanzas (groups of lines) called shabads. The shabads are also called gurbani and are set to ragas (Indian musical notations). When the shabads are sung to music, it is called kirtan. The singers are called ragees.

On festivals and special family occasions, the Guru Granth Sahib is read continuously from beginning to end by a chain of readers. This continuous reading is called Akhand Path. It usually takes about 48 hours. Sehaj Path is a complete reading of the Guru Granth Sahib at intervals (i.e. not continuously), performed at home or at the gurdwara.

Most Sikhs learn passages from the Guru Granth Sahib and recite them daily from memory. Simran Singh, aged four, says:

66 I know the Mool Mantra and two other shabads. 99

He says them when he wakes up in the morning and at night before going to bed. Jasjit Kaur says:

66 I took part in a competition to recite the Japji Sahib, the morning prayer. The competition was for 10 to 14 year-olds. I made a few mistakes so I did not win any prize. I am working hard to memorise it for the next competition. 99

Most Sikhs have their own copy of the Guru Granth Sahib in their home. Because of its importance, Sikhs would not place the Guru Granth Sahib on a shelf, like other books, but keep it in a room of its own. The room is then called a gurdwara, because it houses the Guru Granth Sahib. Almost all Sikhs keep a gutka.

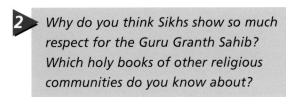

2 *Why do you think Sikhs show so much respect for the Guru Granth Sahib? Which holy books of other religious communities do you know about?*

3 *What is Akhand Path and how is it different from Sehaj Path?*

The Guru writes:

66 Blessed beautiful is the hut
Where the Lord's praise is sung:
Worthless is the palace
Where the Lord is forgotten. 99

[Guru Granth Sahib, page 745]

 4 *Write a summary of what Sikhs believe about the Guru Granth Sahib, and describe how they care for it. (You will see it in many pictures in this book.)*

When they borrow a copy of the Guru Granth Sahib from the gurdwara, to use at a service in their home, Sikhs take special care of the book as they transport it. These Sikhs converted their van to carry the Guru Granth Sahib.

Harinder Singh explains:

66 We have not got a room in our home where we can permanently keep the Guru Granth Sahib. So when my wife and I decided to celebrate our daughter's first birthday at home, we borrowed a copy of the Guru Granth Sahib from the gurdwara. We emptied our sitting room and placed the Guru Granth Sahib there. For that day, our sitting room was the gurdwara. 99

FIFTEEN

The Gurdwara

What places of worship have you visited? In this unit you will learn what distinguishes a Sikh place of worship. You will begin to find out how the Sikh belief in equality is reflected in the Sikh way of worship. This theme is continued in Unit Sixteen.

A Sikh place of worship is called a gurdwara, which means "Guru's door". Many gurdwaras in India were built where special events had taken place in the lives of the Gurus. These are called the historic gurdwaras. But a gurdwara does not have to be a special building. It can be a house or any building large enough for the local community to gather in to worship God. Any place where the Guru Granth Sahib is kept becomes a gurdwara.

Purpose-built gurdwaras may have a dome, but this is not essential. However, whatever the building is like, a gurdwara has the Sikh flag, the "Nishan Sahib", flying outside. The flag is a saffron colour with the Sikh symbol, the khanda, on it.

All gurdwaras have a room where people meet for worship. If the building is large enough, it will have two halls – one for prayer and one for langar (the community dining hall) – plus a kitchen. There is always an area where people can leave their shoes. No one wears shoes in the worship room. In addition, there may be a room to house the library, a classroom for the teaching of Panjabi and music, an office for meetings, and sometimes guest rooms where visitors can stay overnight.

One of the historic gurdwaras in India, the Bangla Sahib in Delhi. It was built on the site where Guru Har Krishan helped the sick, and died himself of smallpox.

▶ *A gurdwara building in London. Is there a gurdwara in your town?*

> **1** ▶ *Why do religious groups have special places to worship?*

Sikhs are told to refrain from taking tobacco and alcohol, and therefore these are not allowed in a gurdwara.

Sikhs and anyone else who wants to worship God can come to a service at the gurdwara and afterwards eat langar (see Unit Sixteen). Prayers are said in the gurdwara every morning and evening. Some gurdwaras are open from dawn to sunset every day, for people to come in to pray. There is no fixed holy day of the week for Sikh worship. In the West, the majority of Sikhs tend to go to services on either Saturdays or Sundays.

2 *Some features are common to the places of worship of all religions (for example, symbols, music, congregation, special people, a large hall). Describe what makes a gurdwara distinct from other places of worship.*

3 *On a visit to a gurdwara, how would you know that women have complete equality with men?*

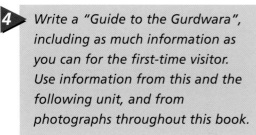

4 *Write a "Guide to the Gurdwara", including as much information as you can for the first-time visitor. Use information from this and the following unit, and from photographs throughout this book.*

Inside a new gurdwara.

A service in the gurdwara is being broadcast live on local radio and commentator Manjit Singh is in the prayer hall to describe the scene:

66 On its platform, the Guru Granth Sahib rests on cushions and is covered with beautiful purple velvet romallas. The canopy over the platform is also purple.

People are coming in and paying their respects to the Guru Granth Sahib by bowing and touching the ground with their forehead. They are placing some money in the box, and some are putting food nearby. The money and food will be used for the langar or for other charitable purposes.

People are sitting down facing the Guru Granth Sahib. Everyone is sitting on the floor, to show that all are equal and that the Guru Granth Sahib is the most important thing in the room. Men and women in this gurdwara sit separately, which is an Indian custom, but there is no hard and fast religious rule about this.

A woman member of the congregation is sitting behind the Guru Granth Sahib, facing the congregation. Occasionally she waves the chouri over it. The chouri is like a fan and is made of yak hair. On a lower platform next to the Guru Granth Sahib musicians are singing a shabad... 99

SIXTEEN

A Service in the Gurdwara

Do you sometimes invite friends home to eat with your family? Is inviting someone to share food a sign that you like that person? In this unit you will learn what happens when Sikhs meet for prayers, and how they eat together after the service, as members of God's family.

Usually, a service in the gurdwara starts with kirtan – the singing of shabads from the Guru Granth Sahib to music played on tabla (drums) and a harmonium – and readings from the Guru Granth Sahib or related religious texts. Any man or woman can perform kirtan but more often it is the ragees, or professional musicians, who play and sing.

After kirtan, a hymn called Anand Sahib, composed by Guru Amar Das, is recited. Then the congregation stands up, hands folded, and listens to the common prayer called the ardas. In this prayer Sikhs first remember God, the Gurus, and the Sikh martyrs; and then they ask for God's blessings on the whole of humanity. There may be prayers for people who are sick, or prayers of thanks for a family's good fortune.

After the prayer, the congregation sits down. The reader of the Guru Granth Sahib opens the book at random and reads a shabad from the page. This is called the hukam, or message for the day.

To finish, krah prashad (the holy sweet) is distributed to everyone present. Krah prashad is a sweet made from flour or semolina, sugar, water, and butter. It is given out at the end of every Sikh service, as a sign of the Guru's blessings and to symbolise that everyone is equal. The service is usually followed by langar.

A Sikh gathering for a service is also called "diwan", and sometimes political and social issues affecting the Sikh community are discussed there. The service can therefore last as long as five or six hours, but people are not expected to stay for the whole time. They can come and go as they want. Services are usually held in Panjabi, the language spoken by most Sikhs. In gurdwaras in Britain, English is often used so that younger people can understand.

 What are the different elements that make up a Sikh service, and in what order do they take place?

People give money and other gifts when they arrive at a service in the gurdwara. Children are taught to take part in all that happens in the service.

2 *Sikhs feel that it is important to go to the gurdwara as they meet like-minded people there. Is it important for you to meet people who have similar views to yours? If so, are there particular places you go to, to meet these people? Write about what you do there.*

3 *Why do Sikhs think it is important for everyone to eat together? Would you share a meal with a stranger or a person you do not get on with?*
Prepare a menu for a meal, making sure that there is something for everyone's taste.

Langar

After a Sikh service everyone is expected to sit and share a meal, which is prepared and served by volunteers from the congregation. Both the meal and the dining hall where it is served are called langar. The idea of langar is to remind Sikhs that all people belong to the same human family and therefore should be treated equally. It was Guru Nanak who started the practice of eating langar.

The langar is run by donations and voluntary labour. Most families from the gurdwara take their turn and consider it an honour to cook and serve langar. The food is always vegetarian so that all can take part. Usually, the meal (which is also called "Guru ka langar") consists of dal (lentils), a vegetable curry, raita (yoghurt), rice, and chapattis.

Helping in the langar is one example of sewa, which means service to others. This is one of the most important principles of Sikhism.

Everyone takes a turn at serving langar.

4 *Write a radio commentary (similar to the one on page 33) describing the scene in a langar hall.*

5 *Make a list of all the ways in which people going to a gurdwara are treated equally.*

Krah prashad is distributed at the end of a Sikh service.

SEVENTEEN

The Naming Ceremony

Do you remember what you did on your last birthday? Why do people mark their birthday as a special day? Do you celebrate other special days in your life? In this and the following three units you will learn how Sikhs celebrate special occasions in their lives.

Sikhs have ceremonies to mark important personal and family events, such as the naming of a child, marriage, and death, and there is a specifically religious ceremony called "Amrit Chhakna", by which a person is initiated as a Sikh. Other occasions that Sikhs celebrate include birthdays and anniversaries, the time a boy starts to wear a turban, moving into a new home, and the starting of a new business.

People taking part in the ceremonies seek God's blessings and renew their spirit of devotion and service. All ceremonies are held in the presence of the Guru Granth Sahib and include shabads, the ardas, hukam, distribution of krah prashad, and langar.

Sikh families welcome the birth of a baby boy or girl as a gift from God and celebrate this at the naming ceremony. Often this ceremony is included as part of a normal service in the gurdwara, or it can be held separately either in the gurdwara or at the family's home.

The majority of Sikh names can be used for both boys and girls. A girl's name is followed by "Kaur" and a boy's name by "Singh", according to an instruction given by Guru Gobind Singh, the tenth Guru. So you might meet a girl called Simran Kaur and a boy called Simran Singh.

Sometimes a family name is added, which could be the name of the area from which the family originated.

Sitting in front of the Guru Granth Sahib for the ceremony at which a name for the baby will be chosen.

1 Sikh boys and girls have similar names. Do you think this causes confusion or does it not matter? If you know any Sikhs, ask them what they think about using the same names for girls and boys.

2 *Explain the meaning of these lines from the hymn on the right:*
"May you love the company of God's people. May God robe you with honour and may your food be the singing of God's praises."

66 When my son was one week old, I went to my parents' house along with my husband and my four-year-old son Simran. We wanted to have a small family gathering for the naming ceremony. As my parents have a gurdwara in their house we held the ceremony there. My mother had completed the Sehaj Path. Simran wanted to act as a granthi but we persuaded him to wait until he was a bit older! He thought that, as it was his baby brother's special day, he should be the one to perform the ceremony.

We sang five hymns, including the one on page 396 of the Guru Granth Sahib, which was composed by Guru Arjan, the fifth Guru, on the birth of his son Hargobind. It reads:

The True God has sent the child. The long lived child has been born by destiny.
The Sikhs sing God's praises in their joy.

In the ardas my husband's and my name were included. Thanks were given to God on our behalf for the gift of the baby, and God's blessings were asked for the baby.

Then, without choosing any particular page, my mother opened the Guru Granth Sahib. I felt quite excited and a bit nervous, but ready to listen to the shabad. We were to choose a name for the baby beginning with the first letter of the first word of the shabad. The first letter was P and everyone started suggesting names. Simran suggested Peanut, which made us laugh a lot, and we used the name for about four weeks until we decided to call him Pavan Singh. 99

This hymn from the Guru Granth Sahib is often recited at the naming ceremony:

66 Dear child, this is your mother's blessing.
May God never be out of your mind even for a minute.
Meditation on God should be your constant concern.
It purges people from all faults.
May God the Guru be kind to you.
May you love the company of God's people.
May God robe you with honour and may your food be the singing of God's praises. 99
[Guru Granth Sahib, page 486]

As Sikh children grow up, they learn about their religion from their family and from people at the gurdwara. Here a group of young people are learning to play the tabla and harmonium.

3 *Why is it important to have a name? Do you like your name? Who chose it and why?*

Marriage

Have you been to
a wedding?
Where was the
ceremony held?
How had the
couple met?
In this unit you will find
out about the Sikh
wedding ceremony and
about Sikh views
on marriage.

The Gurus taught that family life is very important, and marriage is essential to maintain family life.

Most Sikh marriages are assisted marriages, where parents introduce the boy to the girl or vice versa. Even where a boy and girl meet without such an introduction and suggest for themselves that they would like to marry, their families will still be involved. But a marriage cannot take place unless both the boy and the girl agree to it.

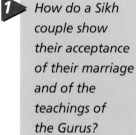

1 *How do a Sikh couple show their acceptance of their marriage and of the teachings of the Gurus? What is the significance of the scarf that the couple hold?*

Mona and Janet were looking through Mona's wedding photographs.
"We hired a hall for my marriage. On the morning of the wedding day, the Guru Granth Sahib was placed in the hall," explained Mona. "I wore pink and my sister and friends accompanied me as I entered the hall and sat next to Harinder, my husband-to-be, who was already sitting in front of the Guru Granth Sahib. Harinder had a scarf round his neck and my father placed one end of it in Harinder's hand and the other in mine. This is a symbol that the couple are being joined and signifies the strong but soft bond between them. We were told to hold our ends of the scarf for the rest of the ceremony."
"What happened next?" asked Janet.
"I better lay the table or there will be no dinner," said Mona. "Here, read this pamphlet which my parents distributed at the time of the wedding, explaining the marriage ceremony."

Sitting in front of the Guru Granth Sahib at the start of the wedding ceremony.

The Sikh marriage ceremony is called Anand Karaj, which means "ceremony of joy". The main part of the ceremony begins when the Guru Granth Sahib is opened and the Lavan (the marriage shabad) is read. This shabad was written by Guru Ram Das, the fourth Guru. It has four verses.

The granthi reads the first verse and then it is sung by the ragees. While the ragees are singing, the couple rise, holding the two ends of the scarf (as explained in Mona's story), and walk clockwise around the Guru Granth Sahib. They

Walking round the Guru Granth Sahib.

walk slowly, with the groom leading. When they get back to their starting position, they bow to the Guru Granth Sahib to show their acceptance of the teachings in the verse. Then they sit down to hear the second verse being read. The reading, singing, walking round the Guru Granth Sahib, and bowing are repeated for each verse. Then the Anand Sahib is read and this concludes the marriage ceremony. The service in the gurdwara continues in the same way as usual.

For Sikhs, a married couple are two equal partners. Sikhism stresses that they should strive towards perfecting a happy union on every level of life: physical, material, intellectual, emotional, and spiritual. Marriage in Sikhism is not considered just a social or civil contract. It is a spiritual union. The love between wife and husband is compared with the love and longing of the human soul for God.

Sikhism gives guidance on responsibilities in marriage and holds that a marriage should be considered as permanent. But the religion and tradition do not rule out the possibility of divorce in the event of a complete breakdown of a marriage.

> 66 They are not man and wife who have only physical contact. Only they are truly wedded who have one spirit in two bodies. 99
>
> [Guru Granth Sahib, page 788]

3 *Write a commentary on a Sikh wedding for the local paper.*

4 *Design an appropriate invitation to a Sikh wedding.*

5 *Do you think that divorce is sometimes necessary? What reasons would make it so? Explain your views.*

2 *A Sikh marriage is between two equal partners, and is for life. What responsibilities do you think the husband and wife have towards each other? What qualities do you think a husband and wife should have to make a successful marriage?*

Amrit Chhakna

Have you or has somebody you know been through a ceremony which marks commitment to a particular belief or society? In this unit you will learn about the initiation ceremony by which Sikhs show their commitment to the faith.

Serving others is an important aspect of life for Sikhs. Because service to society is thought to be most effective if people act as members of a group rather than as individuals, every Sikh is urged to become an active member of the Khalsa Panth, the Sikh community. The ceremony of initiation into the Khalsa Panth is called Amrit Chhakna. It may take place at any time, but Baisakhi is the day when most Sikhs take amrit as that was the day when Guru Gobind Singh introduced the ceremony in 1699 (see Unit Twenty-three).

Any man or woman who is prepared to accept the rules governing the Sikh community has the right to receive amrit. There is no minimum age laid down for taking amrit, but young people are advised to wait until they understand the significance of the vows they will make.

Sometimes amrit is called "khande ka pahul", which means nectar prepared with a double-edged sword. Sugar crystals are dissolved in water by stirring them with the sword while shabads are recited.

At the Amrit Chhakna ceremony, and on other occasions such as festivals, five Sikhs represent the Panj Piare – the first five members of the Khalsa Panth.

"A week before our marriage, my fiance Charan Singh and I decided to take amrit," said Jasbir Kaur. "I was very anxious – actually both of us were. It was an important step we were taking and we were not sure how difficult it would be to practise the promises made."

"On the morning of the day, we met in the gurdwara, both wearing the Five Ks," continued Charan Singh. "I had worn three out of the Five Ks all my life. I had not cut my hair since birth, was given the kara the day I was born, and had worn kachh since I was out of nappies. Wearing the kirpan and kanga in addition to the other three made me reflect on the importance and significance of all five."

"There were about twenty other people who were going to take amrit. We felt a little more confident and less anxious in their company," said Jasbir Kaur.

The Amrit Chhakna ceremony takes place in the gurdwara and always in the presence of the Guru Granth Sahib. It is performed by five people who represent the Panj Piare, the five beloved ones who received amrit from Guru Gobind Singh. These five Sikhs, plus another who reads from the Guru Granth Sahib, are the only people to attend the ceremony, apart from those who are taking amrit. No one else is allowed to observe. At the start of the ceremony, one of the Panj Piare explains the rules and obligations of being a member of the Khalsa Panth. Those taking amrit accept these rules and obligations and then the ardas is said and hukam is read.

Clean water and sugar crystals are put in a steel bowl. As they stir the water with a double-edged sword, the Panj Piare recite five prayers. They and those taking amrit kneel on their right knee, with the left one raised. This is a symbol that they are ready to defend their faith. After the prayers are completed, each person drinks some of the amrit. They receive it in cupped hands and drink it five times. The amrit is also sprinkled five times on both their eyes and their hair. The ceremony ends in the same way as a normal Sikh service.

Sikhs who have taken amrit must always wear the Five Ks, one of which is kes – un-cut hair. Sikh men wear turbans. This is not one of the Five Ks but is an important symbol of the Sikh faith. The turban is a piece of cloth about five metres long that is wound tightly around the head.

Un-cut hair (kes) is one of the Five Ks, and the comb (kanga) worn to keep it neat is another. This Sikh boy has never had his hair cut.

2 In a group, discuss and write down some of the difficulties a young Sikh would face in wearing the Five Ks in your school.

The three others of the Five Ks are kachh (shorts), kara (the bangle), and kirpan (the sword). There is more about the Five Ks in Unit One and in Unit Twenty-three.

1 Do you wear a badge or tie or other item of clothing that shows that you belong to a club or organisation? What is the purpose of wearing it? Does the club or organisation have rules that you need to obey?
Do you feel committed to observing those rules? Write some rules that you think it would be good for members of a group of friends to obey.

3 With a partner, brainstorm and write down the advantages for a Sikh of wearing the Five Ks.

twenty

Death

Sikhs are told to accept God's will at the time of a death in the family, to avoid showing grief, and to find comfort in reading the Guru Granth Sahib. They should remember the Gurus' teachings that:

"The dawn of a new day is the message of a sunset.
Earth is not the permanent home."

"Life is like a shadow on the wall."
(Guru Granth Sahib, page 793)

The Sikh Gurus taught that, for those who have lived truly good lives, death could be a liberation from the impermanent, changing world. The souls of those people find union with God.

> 66 Worldly souls who scorn God's sweetness suffer pain because of their conceit.
> The thorn of death pricks deeper and deeper.
> Those who love God's sacred name shall break the bonds of birth and death.
> Thus they find the eternal one; thus they win supreme honour.
> I am poor and humble, keep me and save me, God most high.
> Grant the aid that your name can give me.
> Grant me the peace and joy.
> Grant the joy of serving all who praise God's name. 99
>
> *[Guru Granth Sahib, page 13]*

Sikhs believe in the transmigration of souls: that when a person dies, the soul moves on to another body. This can happen over and over again. Human birth is an opportunity to become united with God, by living a good life. If this opportunity is lost, the soul goes back into the cycle of birth and death.

Sikhs are taught that humans have free will to be good or bad. The family into which a person is born is decided according to karma (the person's good or bad actions in the previous life), but a person can always come closer to God by leading a good life following the Gurus' teachings.

Sikhs believe in reincarnation: that a person is born again. In the same way as you go to sleep at the end of the day and wake up the next morning, at the end of one life you die and are reborn in another. It is natural for people who are left to feel sorrow, but they should remember that the person who has died has gone on to another life. Before they go to sleep Sikhs read the Kirtan Sohila, which is also the prayer used at funerals.

Sikhs always cremate their dead. In India, where arrangements for refrigeration are not common, the body is cremated within a day or so of death. In Britain the time between death and cremation depends on the availability of the crematorium.

On the day of the cremation, the body is washed and dressed in the Five Ks and taken home for people to pay their last respects. Then it is taken to the crematorium in a procession or motorcade. The coffin is often carried by male relatives and friends but women may carry it as well. All the family and friends go to the crematorium, where the Kirtan Sohila is recited and the ardas is said to ask for peace for the departed soul.

After the cremation, the ashes are usually thrown in a river or the sea. Some Sikhs in Britain take the ashes to scatter in Punjab.

Sikhs are forbidden to put up any headstones or other memorials to people who have died. They believe that people should be remembered by the good things they did during their life.

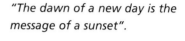

"The dawn of a new day is the message of a sunset".

1 What do you understand by the words "transmigration" and "reincarnation"?

2 Reflect on the Gurus' sayings about death and draw a picture to represent one of the images they suggest.

3 Imagine that you have attended a Sikh funeral. Write a letter to the bereaved.

4 Think of some ways in which a person's life could be remembered, other than by putting up a headstone or memorial.

❝ When my mother died I was very sad, and could not stop crying. My father asked me to sit with him and listen to the Sehaj Path. The hymns made me understand that everyone has to go and my mother has done her duty in this world and has gone to the next. ❞

[Parveen Singh]

❝ After the funeral of my grandfather we went to the gurdwara for the funeral service called the Bhog ceremony, the completion of life's journey. After the kirtan, ardas was said for my grandfather, asking God to give him a place with him. Krah prashad was distributed. We all had langar and went home a little sad and tired. ❞

[Rema Kaur]

Gurus' Days

There are many Sikh festivals, called "Gurpurabs" (Gurus' days), that celebrate events in the Gurus' lives. Only the main ones are described in this book. The celebrations usually take place on the weekend following the actual date being remembered.

All the festivals are celebrated with Akhand Path, the continuous reading aloud of the Guru Granth Sahib, which takes approximately forty-eight hours. It is timed to finish on the morning of the festival day. A number of people do the reading, each taking over from the one before so that there is no break and each reading for a maximum of two hours at a time. These people can be any members of the Sikh community who can read the Guru Granth Sahib clearly and accurately. Sikhs make a special effort to go to listen to the reading, and langar is served throughout the time that it is happening, so many volunteers are needed to cook, serve, and clean up. The completion of Akhand Path is followed by singing of shabads and talks on the significance of the day. Then the Sikh service continues as usual.

As well as saying prayers in the gurdwara, Sikhs sometimes take part in processions on festival days. They give money and other gifts to charitable organisations, and they participate in sewa, which means serving the needy. Some Sikh doctors give free blood tests on Gurpurabs, dentists offer free dental check-ups, and other Sikhs may cook and distribute free food to the poor.

A martial arts display as part of a Sikh festival procession in Britain.

1 *Write a postcard to a friend describing a Sikh festival procession.*

2 *Sikhs are encouraged to celebrate Gurpurabs by serving others (sewa). Suggest some acts of service that a boy or girl could do.*

The Birthdays of Guru Nanak and Guru Gobind Singh

On the Western calendar, the birthday of Guru Nanak, the first Sikh Guru, generally falls in October or November and that of Guru Gobind Singh, the tenth Guru, in December or January. Both days are celebrated with great spirit. In Punjab, gurdwaras, shops, offices, and homes are lit with candles. Children are given new clothes and have a day off school to join in the processions.

In India, and in many places in Britain where there are large numbers of Sikhs, people process through the streets. The procession is led by five people representing the Panj Piare, the five men who were the first to join the Khalsa Panth. Behind them comes a beautifully decorated float carrying the Guru Granth Sahib. Everyone following sings hymns written by the Guru whose birthday is being celebrated. School music bands often join in, and other young people give displays of martial arts. People who go to watch are usually given sweets or fruit and soft drinks.

Guru Nanak's and Guru Gobind Singh's birthdays are celebrated by Sikhs all over the world, but special celebrations are held in the Gurus' respective birth places, Nankana Sahib in Pakistan and Patna in north-eastern India.

> 66 It is important for me to celebrate the Gurus' birthdays. On these days I think especially about the Gurus' teachings and reflect on what I am doing to see if I am really practising what the Gurus taught. 99
>
> [Pavan Kaur]

> 66 It is easy to recite prayers parrot fashion, but it is hard to practise the teachings contained in the prayers. On Gurpurabs I listen to the life stories of the Gurus and I get inspired and want to follow in their footsteps. 99
>
> [Jit Singh]

Celebrating the Guru's birthday in Anandpur, India.

TWENTY-TWO

The Martyrdoms of Guru Arjan and Guru Tegh Bahadur

In this unit you will find out how Sikhs commemorate the two Gurus who were put to death for their belief in religious tolerance.

Guru Arjan Dev is made to sit on red-hot metal, and hot sand is poured over him. He still would not give up his belief in religious tolerance.

The Martyrdom of Guru Arjan Dev

In 1606 Guru Arjan, the fifth Guru, was tortured to death. The Mughal ruler had ordered the Guru's arrest and said that he would be freed only if he stopped preaching his religion and paid 200,000 rupees. The Guru's reply was that he could never stop preaching his religion and that, if he had such a huge sum of money, he would give it to the poor.

For three days in the hottest month of May, the Guru was locked in a cell without any food or water. On the fourth day he was put in a barrel of hot water. As this was not enough to break his resolve, on the fifth day hot sand was poured onto his naked body, and on the sixth day he was made to sit on a red-hot iron plate. Then the Guru was pushed into the river where he drowned and was washed away. Not once did the Guru complain or ask for mercy. He repeated over and over again the name of God and said, "Your Will is sweet to me."

The Guru was punished for teaching tolerance: that all people had the right to worship as they chose and that no religion had a monopoly of the truth.

In keeping with the Guru's teachings on tolerance, Sikhs mark the anniversary of his death by setting up roadside stalls, wherever practicable, to serve cool drinks to passers-by. Sikhs remember the thirst and suffering of Guru Arjan Dev by looking to the thirst of others – whatever their race and creed.

1 *What do you think of the way in which Sikhs commemorate the martyrdom of Guru Arjan Dev? What might be the thoughts of someone serving the drinks, and someone receiving a drink?*

The Martyrdom of Guru Tegh Bahadur

In 1675 Guru Tegh Bahadur, the ninth Sikh Guru, was martyred for his belief. India was then ruled by the Mughal emperor Aurengzeb, who was forcing Hindus to accept Islam and killing many who refused.

Sikhs all over the world commemorate the Guru's death not by expressing grief but by Akhand Path and prayers, in the same way as on other Gurpurabs (see Unit Twenty-one).

2 *Look at the story of Guru Tegh Bahadur. Do you think that any people today suffer for their beliefs, or for helping others?*

The story of Guru Tegh Bahadur.

Some Brahmins (members of the Hindu priestly class) from Kashmir approached Guru Tegh Bahadur.

"We know you don't agree with many of our practices, but you have always spoken about people's right to follow their own way of life. We appeal to you for help to stop the Mughal atrocities."

The Guru knew that any action he took to help the Brahmins would put his own life at risk, but he agreed to help.

"Go and tell Emperor Aurengzeb that if the Guru accepts Islam, the whole of the Hindu community too will become Muslims without further resistance."

The emperor was delighted. He thought this would be an easy way of converting the whole Hindu population of India to Islam. So he called the Guru to Delhi.

"I am happy with my own religion."

"If you become a Muslim you can have a beautiful palace to live in and great riches to spend as you like."

"Islam is a wonderful religion. You should adopt it."

"I don't need any riches. My needs are very simple."

"If you don't listen to me, you will be tortured and then put to death!"

"Never seek to intimidate others, nor be cowed by another's might!"

The Guru and his companions were taken away to be tortured and then, on a cold winter day, the Guru was publicly beheaded by the orders of the emperor for his stand on religious freedom.

TWENTY-THREE

Baisakhi and Diwali

Baisakhi

Baisakhi is a New Year festival in the Sikh calendar. On the Western calendar it usually falls in April. It was at the time of Baisakhi that Guru Gobind Singh conducted the first Amrit ceremony in 1699, and nowadays the Amrit ceremony (see Unit Nineteen) is performed at most gurdwaras on this day.

A tradition on Baisakhi day is to renew the Nishan Sahib, the flag outside the gurdwara. A service led by five Sikhs representing the Panj Piare is held outside. The flag post is taken down and the "chola" (the cloth covering the post) is removed. The post is cleaned, covered with a new chola, and re-hoisted. The ceremony is completed by saying the ardas.

Another tradition for Baisakhi is to hold competitions in sports, martial arts, music, poetry, public speaking, and many other areas.

Diwali

Diwali means the festival of lights. On Diwali day Sikhs celebrate the arrival in Amritsar of Guru Hargobind, the sixth Guru, after his release from a Mughal prison. There are firework displays, and the whole of the Golden Temple complex is illuminated. The historic treasures there and weapons used by the Gurus are exhibited for the festival.

Guru Hargobind was imprisoned by the Mughal emperor Jehangir, on the charge of raising an army and committing treason. On examination, the charge was found to be baseless and the Guru was released. But fifty-two Hindu princes were being held in the prison, for political reasons, and Guru Hargobind believed that they should not be punished in this way. He refused to leave the prison unless the princes were also freed.

Royal officials reported this to the emperor who agreed to release the princes on one condition. Only those princes who could pass through the prison gates holding on to the Guru's cloak could go free. This sounded impossible, as there was a very narrow passage on the way to the main gate out of the prison. Only one person at a time could go through. However, the Guru asked for a cloak to be made with fifty-two tassels of different lengths. Then all the princes were able to hold on to the different tassels of the cloak and so gain their freedom.

Guru Hargobind leads the fifty-two Hindu princes out of the prison.

On Baisakhi day in 1699, over 20,000 Sikhs gathered in Anandpur to meet Guru Gobind Singh. The Guru appeared holding a naked sword and said, "I need a Sikh who is willing to give his life for God and the Guru."

A stunned silence followed. The Guru repeated his request twice more. At last a Sikh came forward.

The Guru took him to a nearby tent, then reappeared, his sword apparently dripping with blood, and asked for another Sikh. Again the Guru took the second Sikh to the tent and returned asking for another. This happened three more times so that, in the end, the congregation had seen five men offer themselves and be taken into the tent.

After the fifth time, the Guru did not come back for a while. When he did, all five men were with him. The Guru explained that he had been testing their courage and willingness to die for their faith and the Guru. The Sikh community had passed the test. He called the five men Panj Piare (Five Beloved Ones).

Then the Guru prepared amrit, a mixture of sugar and water which he stirred with a khanda, a two-edged sword. His wife Mata Sundri brought the sugar crystals to sweeten the amrit and the Guru said, "Your contribution has made the ceremony complete."

The Guru asked the Panj Piare to give him amrit, showing that all people, including the Guru, are equal before God. Then amrit was given to thousands of the people present, as a sign that they accepted the basic Sikh principles of belief in one God, equality of all people, and respect and tolerance towards all. It was also on this day that Guru Gobind Singh asked Sikhs to wear the Five Ks.

1 ▶ *Why were the five men called Beloved Ones? How did Guru Gobind Singh demonstrate that all people are equal before God?*

2 ▶ *If you were in a position to help others out of danger, would you be more prepared to help some kinds of people than others? Would you risk your own freedom to help others?*

3 ▶ *Sikhs are taught to have faith in God and to stand up for their principles, even if this causes them to suffer. Explain how the two stories here convey those messages.*

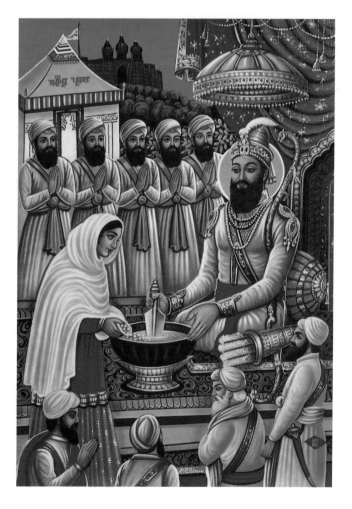

Guru Gobind Singh stirs the amrit as his wife, Mata Sundri, pours in the sugar crystals.

49

Family and Home Life

The Sikh way of life can first be learned and practised in the home.

After a morning bath or shower, Sikhs start the day by meditating on God. In some religions meditation involves special postures or exercises or concentrating on a particular object. But Sikh meditation is not like this. If they are short of time, Sikhs can recite the Japji Sahib, the morning prayer, at the same time as they are getting ready or doing household chores. Very young children are encouraged to repeat "WAHEGURU" (The Wonderful Lord), a popular Sikh name for God.

There are also set passages for evening and bedtime prayers, which Sikhs say each day.

1 *What do you learn about Sikh family life from the descriptions people give on these two pages? In what ways is your own family life similar or different?*

66 When I go to my grandmother's house, we sometimes go in the special room called the gurdwara and sing hymns. I usually wave the chouri over the Guru Granth Sahib and recite the two hymns I have memorised. Sometimes my uncle's family joins us as well, and my cousin Kirat gives the krah prashad and I give out the tissues for wiping our hands afterwards. 99

[Simran Singh]

During the time of Guru Nanak, society thought highly of yogis (holy men), who believed that they could find God by concentrating solely on Him. They cut themselves off from their families and normal everyday life and work, because they thought that all these things prevented spiritual union with God. Guru Nanak remarked that these men still needed the help of ordinary families to live a full life:

66 For food and clothes, these holy men still go from door to door begging. 99

[Guru Granth Sahib, page 879]

The Guru taught his Sikhs to live in the world but not be corrupted by it. He taught:

66 As the lotus in the pool and the fowl in the stream remain dry, so a person should live untouched by the world. 99

[Guru Granth Sahib, page 938]

Sikhs are taught to stand clear of corruption, as the lotus flower stands clear of the water.

A Sikh family in the south of England.

2 ▶ *Write a report for the local newspaper about Sikh family life.*

The family is the basic unit of the Sikh community, where lessons in love and respect are learned. Parents are told that children are a gift from God that they are entrusted to look after. Boys and girls are treated equally.

The Guru reminds children that when they were small and helpless, their parents did their duty and cared for them as best they could.

66 We have a big family. My grandad and grandma live with us. One of my uncles and his family live next door, and the other uncle and his family live ten houses away. Quite often we all get together for dinner and I have great fun with my cousins. We make such a lot of noise that our parents and grandparents get fed up. Birthday parties are such fun. Jivan, my oldest cousin, is teaching me some magic tricks. 99

[Harinder]

Mona wrote in her diary:

66 I went to the gurdwara with my family. My grandmother showed me the paintings about the lives of the Gurus. I saw Guru Nanak feeding the hungry, Guru Hargobind coming out of jail followed by fifty-two princes, Guru Gobind Singh asking for a Sikh, and many more. I enjoyed looking at the paintings. Then I went to my Sunday school to learn Panjabi. 99

66 My mum told me that, when we came from Kenya, my grandmother used to look after me, while my mum was at work teaching history. Now my mum doesn't go to work because she looks after my grandmother. I help push my grandmother's wheelchair and take her out at weekends. Sometimes my aunt and uncle and cousins come and take her to the gurdwara, as they have a bigger car and the wheelchair can fit in better. 99

[Satwant]

Therefore, when their parents are old and cannot look after themselves, it is the children's duty to care for them. The Guru says:

"Son, why do you quarrel with your father? Due to him you have grown to this age."
(Guru Granth Sahib, page 1200)

The Sikh Gurus recommended family life. All of them except Guru Har Krishan, who died when he was eight, were married and had children. This is Guru Gobind Singh with his four sons.

TWENTY-FIVE

Women

Think of examples of when you are treated with the same respect as other people. What effect does it have? Does being treated as an equal give you confidence to perform a task well? In this unit you will learn about Sikh teachings on the equality of women with men.

From the beginning, Sikhism gave women equality with men in all of the religion's affairs. Men and women attend services as equal members of the congregation. Both conduct services. They work side by side in preparing and serving krah prashad and langar. They share equal responsibilities in all the social and cultural activities of the gurdwara. Sikh women and men participate on equal terms as presidents, secretaries, and members of gurdwaras and Sikh organisations.

By recommending family life as the place to find God, the Gurus gave women an important status. This was in contrast to the idea of the holy men of their time (see Unit Twenty-four), who saw women as evil and a hindrance to men who wanted to serve God. The Guru writes:

"Blessed is the woman who creates life."
(Guru Granth Sahib, page 32)

The Gurus did not say that men and women should play exactly the same roles in every area of life. They taught that men and women should respect and value equally the different roles that each undertakes. In the Sikh marriage vows, the emphasis is on mutual faithfulness, and this again gives women equality with men.

In the world of work, Sikh men and women are free to follow any profession they want. There should be no preconceived ideas about certain roles or professions being more suitable for one or the other. The Gurus respected the choice of

Guru Amar Das forbade his Sikhs to take part in any of the social customs that showed that women had inferior status to men. These included such cruel customs as killing baby girls, and Sati, where a widow killed herself on her husband's funeral pyre. Also the Guru forbade Sikh women to wear purdah (the veil), which was a sign of women's lower status.

Guru Amar Das included three women in a total of twenty-two leaders whom he chose to teach Sikhism, and he established fifty-two study circles to educate women.

1 ▶ *Do you think it is fair that women should have equality with men? Explain your views.*

Maharani Sada Kaur was an important leader of Sikh troops in the late eighteenth century.

Women in the gurdwara.

Guru Gobind Singh gave amrit to women as well as men and instructed both men and women to wear the Five Ks. He gave men the title "Singh" and women the title "Kaur" – and so a Sikh woman does not have to take her father's or husband's name; she is always called Kaur, implying that she is a person in her own right.

Men and women take part in building a new gurdwara in Delhi.

some women to become soldiers, to fight for their religion. Other women during and after the time of the Gurus became political and religious leaders.

Today, in many cases, Sikh women do not come forward to become leaders of their community. There are many reasons for this, but the main one is probably that Sikhs are a minority in countries whose traditions do not stress the equality of women, or even disagree with it.

At the time of Guru Nanak, other religions in India treated women as inferior to men. The Guru condemned society's low opinion of women and said:

❝ In a woman we are conceived,
    From a woman we are born.
It is with woman we are betrothed and married.
It is woman that we befriend, it is a woman who
    keeps the race going.
Why should we call her inferior, who gives
    birth to great men?
From a woman a woman is born
None is born without a woman. ❞

[Guru Granth Sahib, page 473]

2 ▶ Do you think women and men have equality? If not, make a list of the areas where inequalities exist and say how you think complete equality could be brought about.

3 ▶ Write a list of what the Gurus did to make women equal with men.

4 ▶ In Britain, the Equal Opportunities Act was passed to make sure that all people have the same rights, regardless of their sex or race. Do you think legislation like this is necessary to ensure that all members of a society have equality?

TWENTY-SIX

Rules To Live By

The Sikh Gurus taught that it is people's behaviour, rather than what they say, that makes them good or bad. How do you think you judge people? In this and the following unit you will find out how Sikhs try to ensure that they live good lives.

The Sikh ideal is to lead life according to these three rules:

▶ Nam Japna – remembering God
▶ Kirat Karni – earning one's living by honest means and hard work
▶ Vand Chhakna – sharing with others who are less fortunate than yourself.

Nam Japna is meditation on the qualities of God as described in the Guru Granth Sahib. Meditation does not just mean closing one's eyes and saying shabads. It is important to understand the words and to act upon what they teach. Remembering God should lead Sikhs to live a good life and to work for the good of society. They pray together with other Sikhs at home and in the gurdwara, because meeting with people who have similar views helps give confidence to practise the religion.

Kirat Karni means working hard to earn one's living. Sikhism encourages family life and this brings many responsibilities. Sikhs must balance worship and meditation with honest work and good deeds. A holy person is one who tries to serve others selflessly. The Guru says:

Everyone takes part in cleaning the pavements at the Golden Temple.

"He alone has found the right way who eats what he earns through hard work and shares his earnings with others."
(Guru Granth Sahib, page 1245)

According to Sikhism, all work is noble, including tasks that may be thought low or menial. Rich and poor Sikhs alike learn to do "lowly" jobs when they go to the gurdwara: for example, cleaning visitors' shoes, fanning the congregation in the intense heat of India, cleaning dishes, cooking food, scrubbing floors, or any repair jobs. Sikhs are often reminded of the way Guru Gobind Singh refused a cup of water from a young man whose soft hands indicated that he had never done a day's work.

Sikhs should earn their living by honest means, working hard, and taking a fair profit. They should use their wealth for practical purposes, and not let wealth dominate their lives.

Guru Nanak compares the bread offered by Lalo and by Bhago.

1 ▸ Discuss the Sikh idea that one should use wealth for practical purposes but not let it dominate one's life.
Think of people you know or have heard about who have been "unaffected" by their wealth, and write about some of them.

2 ▸ In Bhago's position, how would you have responded?
Do you think it is important to help others?
If so, how do you help others?
Make a list of things a friend could do to help you.

On one of his journeys Guru Nanak reached Emnabad, where he accepted an invitation to stay with a humble carpenter called Lalo. Bhago, who was a wealthy man, decided to give a feast and invited all the rich and famous people he could think of, including Guru Nanak. When the Guru did not attend, Bhago asked: "Why have you refused to attend my feast?"

The Guru replied, "Lalo's simple bread is earned by honest labour, but you have grown rich by exploiting and taking advantage of the poor. Your food is stained with the blood of the poor."

"Nonsense!" shouted Bhago angrily. The Guru smiled, and then, according to legend, took a piece of bread from Lalo's house in one hand and a piece of bread from Bhago's house in the other. He squeezed them both. Milk dripped from Lalo's bread and blood from Bhago's. The rich man realised his mistake and promised the Guru to devote the rest of his life to helping those in need.

In need of correction

Mr Singh has a factory where he employs over 100 people. He made over £500,000 profit last year. He won't employ women, because he might then have to pay maternity benefits, and he recently refused to give a day's leave to a worker who wanted to take his child to hospital for treatment. He would not employ Muslims because they take time off for prayers. He pays lower wages to employees over fifty than to others, because he knows the older ones would find it difficult to get any other jobs.

 Make a list of the ways in which Mr Singh is not behaving as a Sikh should. Suggest three actions which should be taken to correct matters.

Vand Chhakna and Sewa

Vand Chhakna is the third rule by which Sikhs try to live their lives. It means sharing what they have with others. Part of this sharing is sewa, serving others. In this unit you will learn about these Sikh practices and think about the importance of caring for people less fortunate than you.

Following the third Sikh rule may mean giving money, or giving time, or using one's skills or expertise to help others. It involves helping everyone, not only other Sikhs. The idea of sewa has led gurdwaras in India, East Africa, and other countries where Sikhs have been settled for some time, to open hospitals where free treatment is given to anyone who cannot afford to pay. Free accommodation is also provided. To discourage people from taking advantage of these things in a lazy way, everyone is reminded to participate in sewa, even if it is simply doing jobs in the langar.

Preparing and serving langar are important experiences from which Sikhs can learn about sewa, and even very young children are encouraged to play some part.

Bhai Kanaya gives water to a wounded soldier.

1 ▶ *What do we learn from the story of Bhai Kanaya? Make a list of things you can do to help a sick person.*

When the Mughal emperor's forces were attacking Guru Gobind Singh, the Sikhs gave Kanaya the duty of providing water to the wounded. One day he was captured by some Sikh guards and brought to the Guru's tent. "He is a traitor. He has been helping the enemy," one of them reported.

Kanaya explained: "I am a water carrier. It's my duty to take water to the wounded and dying. So when the battle ended today, as usual, I took water round to the injured soldiers."

"But he was giving water to Muslim soldiers as well," said the guard angrily. The Guru asked if this was true and Kanaya said, "When I was taking water round the battlefield, I saw no Muslims and no Sikhs, no friends, no enemies. I saw only God's people. I was practising what you taught us."

"You are a true Sikh," said the Guru, "and a real brother to all. We will from now on call you Bhai, a brother." Thus the Guru blessed him for his true spirit of service to God's creation. He ordered that Bhai Kanaya should also be given ointment, so that he could go and heal the wounds of injured soldiers, both Sikh and Muslim.

Bhagat Puran Singh takes someone to the pingalwara.

 2 *Plan a day's outing to the seaside for forty people. People will have their lunch at local eating places and you will all be back home before dinner. Make a list of things to do beforehand and on the day of the outing. Include what you need to take with you.*

Sikhs are often reminded of the selfless service of Bhagat Puran Singh. When he was still in his teens, his father's banking business collapsed and so he moved to the city to look for a job. There he stayed in a gurdwara where free food and lodgings were provided to people in need. Impressed by the service given by the gurdwara, Puran Singh spent most of his time carrying the sick to the nearby hospital and taking them food from the gurdwara langar.

After the partition of India in 1947, Puran Singh moved to Amritsar and carried on serving the sick. With the help of donations from Sikhs, he opened the "pingalwara", a house for crippled people. Puran Singh was often seen carrying a disabled or sick person on his shoulders to the pingalwara. Not only did he provide medication to alleviate people's physical suffering but he also gave love and care to those whom society rejected.

66 We took some old people from the local Day Centre on an outing to the seaside. Some of them had not been to the sea for a long time. They enjoyed the outing, but I enjoyed it even more to see lots of people, White, Black, and Asian, all enjoying themselves together. It was my best day out ever. We have asked the gurdwara people to arrange these outings more often during the holidays, and our group will help. 99

[Jasjit]

3 *What do you learn about the Sikh view of sewa from the stories of Bhai Kanaya and Bhagat Puran Singh?*
Make a poster illustrating the Sikh view of sewa. Ask a friend what the poster conveys to him or her.

57

TWENTY-EIGHT

Nature

In this unit you will learn what the Gurus said about nature, and you will think about how Sikh ideas can be applied to today's environmental issues.

Sikhs believe that God is the creator of the universe, of everything known and unknown. The universe was and is still being created at God's will.

> "God created nature.
> Seated in nature,
> God watches the fullness of the creation."
> (Guru Granth Sahib, page 463)

The spirit of God is said to be present in nature.

> "In Nature we see God,
> In Nature we hear God speak,
> Nature inspires devotion.
> In Nature is the essence of joy and peace.
> (Guru Granth Sahib, page 464)

Sikhs are taught that God's creation is limitless. In this context, the Earth is so small that its destruction would make hardly any difference to God. But human beings would suffer from the planet's destruction. Human beings are free to make choices and are responsible for their actions. It is important that their decisions and actions remain within the laws of nature. Sikhs are told to live according to God's will. Breaking God's laws either knowingly or unknowingly causes pain and suffering.

Sikhs assessing an environmental project in Punjab.

The Sikh Gurus themselves worked actively to use God's gift of the environment to serve others, in a way that preserved the balance of nature. After his missionary journeys, Guru Nanak settled to work as a farmer. The majority of Sikhs in Punjab choose to be farmers. They have converted Punjab, a small area in India, into the "bread-basket" of the whole country. They have planted trees by roads and canals, and they own flower and fruit orchards.

Indarjit Singh put forward some Sikh ideas about nature to a group of young people who visited the gurdwara:

❝ We human beings cannot understand the vastness of our universe. It is our responsibility to protect and save the environment from destruction. God is like a benevolent parent who has provided for everyone. God's creation must not be abused for selfish purposes and we should use all the resources that have been given to us wisely, with care and compassion. Plant and animal conservation is every Sikh's religious duty. The environment survives only if the balance designed by God is maintained. ❞

 Write and perform an interview, in which one of Guru Har Rai's companions tells an interviewer about the incident with the bush of flowers.

The Gurus used examples from nature to convey lessons about life. Guru Nanak explained that size and might are nothing:

❝ The simal tree is huge and tall, But if one comes to it with hope of gain, what will one get? Its fruit is tasteless, its flowers have no fragrance, its leaves are of no use. Nanak says, humility and sweetness are the essence of virtue and goodness. ❞

Guru Har Rai and the flowers.

Once Guru Har Rai, the seventh Guru, was walking with some Sikhs in a garden. He was admiring the beautiful plants, trees, and flowers when a sudden puff of wind caused the tassels of his cloak to get entangled in a bush of flowers. Petals fell on the ground and the Guru was upset that he had carelessly destroyed some flowers. His companions were surprised. "There are many more flowers in the garden," they said. "Why worry about a few?" The Guru reminded them that no one has a right to destroy even one flower; all of God's creation should be respected.

 Make a list of things that you can do to help conserve the natural environment and prevent it from being harmed.

TWENTY-NINE

Sikhs in Britain

In this unit you will find out why many Sikhs moved from India and East Africa and made Britain their home. You will think about the effects that moving from one's homeland may have.

The families of most of the 400,000 Sikhs in Britain today originate from India or East Africa.

In 1947, British rule in India came to an end and some provinces of India became the separate country of Pakistan, under Muslim rule. Over two million Sikhs left their homes and land in Pakistan and many moved to Britain, where there were job opportunities.

It was in the 1960s and 1970s that most Sikhs left India to come to Britain. These people found work in factories, often doing jobs that white people did not want to do. Some started their own businesses, on a small scale, selling things from door to door or on a market stall.

By the late 1990s, most Sikh families in Britain have been settled in the country for more than thirty years. About two-thirds of the total Sikh population of Britain today was born in this country.

Wherever in Britain Sikhs settled, they collected money in order to build gurdwaras or buy existing buildings that they could convert into gurdwaras. There are now about 300 gurdwaras in Britain. The Sikh community (Panth) in each area gathers to discuss important issues concerning Sikhs: for example, what to do when a head teacher refused to let a Sikh boy enter his school if he was wearing a turban; or what to do when crash helmets were made compulsory for motor cyclists and Sikhs could not wear these as well as their turbans. (The Sikh community was able to get the law changed, to exempt Sikhs.)

Sikhs outside their gurdwara, at the Baisakhi festival (see Unit Twenty-three). They are lowering the Nishan Sahib (flag), to replace it with a new one.

In a letter to a friend in Canada, Mina explained her background:

66 In 1920 my grandparents went to Uganda in East Africa. At that time the British ruled both India and East Africa and they took skilled workers from India to help build railways in East Africa. One of my grandfathers was a surveyor.

My parents were both born in Uganda. My mother worked as a teacher and my father as a structural engineer. My brother and I were also both born in Uganda. But in 1972, General Idi Amin, who was then President of Uganda, forced all Asians to leave the country. We left our homes and all our other possessions and came to England. Even today, I can picture the doll I left behind. 99

The Sikh community realises that its children should have at least a basic knowledge and understanding of Sikhism. Sikhs – especially males with their turbans – are a very visible minority and so they can, and do, meet prejudice in schools and later on at work.

Having a real understanding of their religious tradition gives young people greater strength to deal with such prejudice. They also need much support from their family and the community to help them practise their religion without losing self-esteem.

> 66 I go to India every two to three years for a reunion with my mother, sisters and brothers, and their families. But for my two daughters, who were born in England, trips to Punjab are simply holidays. They have very little in common with their cousins in Punjab. 99
>
> [Jasbir Kaur]

> 66 I would go home and plead with my mother to have my hair cut, so there would be one less level of teasing and bullying. She would always say no, that is my identity; hundreds and thousands of Sikhs have died fighting for the right to practise their religion. 99
>
> [Ravinder]

> 66 I don't go to the gurdwara regularly, as I can't understand the service which is in Panjabi. Occasionally, when there are talks in English, I do go and learn about my religion. I went on Guru Nanak's birthday and enjoyed the talk. 99
>
> [Mandeep]

> 66 It was very difficult when my son used to come home pleading with me to cut his hair. I spoke to about twenty other parents, and they all talked about the sleepless nights they had thinking of ways to give their sons confidence and self-esteem so that they could cope with the bullying and prejudice of their peers. 99
>
> [Kawaljit Kaur, president of her local gurdwara]

Young Sikhs at a Panjabi class run by the gurdwara.

2 ▶ Why do you think young Sikhs feel the need to learn Panjabi?

3 ▶ Look again at what you wrote about your knowledge of Sikhs when you first started to use this book (see question 1 on page 4). How have your ideas and impressions changed, now that you know more?

1 ▶ Why do you think people like to know the history of their family? Do you know where your family comes from, and do you sometimes visit that place?

61

Glossary

Adi Granth The name by which the Guru Granth Sahib was first known

Akal Purukh "The eternal one" – a name often used for God

Akhand Path Continuous reading of the Guru Granth Sahib

amrit Literally, nectar. It is made by stirring sugar crystals into water with a double-edged sword, while certain passages from the scriptures are recited.

ardas A formal prayer offered at all religious services and ceremonies

chouri A fan made of yak hair or nylon, which is waved over the Guru Granth Sahib to show respect for the scripture

diwan A gathering for worship

granthi A specially appointed reader of the Guru Granth Sahib who officiates at ceremonies

gurdwara The Sikh place of worship

Gurmukhi Meaning "from the Guru's mouth", this is the name given to the script in which the Sikh scriptures and the Panjabi language are written

hukam A reading taken at random from the Guru Granth Sahib and understood as guidance. "Hukam" means "God's will".

Kaur Literally, princess. The name is given to every female Sikh, following an instruction from Guru Gobind Singh.

Khalsa Panth The Sikh community

khanda The double-edged sword used in the initiation ceremony (Amrit Chhakna). It is the symbol on the Sikh flag, the Nishan Sahib.

Kirat Karni Earning one's living by one's own honest efforts – one of the three rules by which Sikhs try to live their lives

krah prashad A sweet food made with equal quantities of flour or semolina, sugar, and butter or ghee (purified butter). It is shared at the end of Sikh gatherings, to symbolise equality.

langar Meaning "Guru's kitchen", this word is used both for the kitchen/dining hall at the gurdwara and for the food that is served there

Lavan The marriage hymn. The word is also used for the part of the marriage ceremony where the couple walk round the Guru Granth Sahib.

Nam Japna Meditation on God's name, using passages from the Guru Granth Sahib. This is one of the three rules by which Sikhs try to live their lives.

Nishan Sahib The Sikh flag flown at gurdwaras and other Sikh buildings. It is saffron-coloured, triangular, and has the khanda symbol on it.

Panjabi The language spoken by Punjabis

Panj Piare The "Five Beloved Ones" – the first five people initiated into the Sikh community (Khalsa Panth) by Guru Gobind Singh

Panth The Sikh community (shortened form of "Khalsa Panth")

patka A head covering worn by boys before they start to wear a turban

Punjab The area of India where Sikhism originated

ragees Sikh musicians who sing compositions from the Guru Granth Sahib

romallas Cloths used as coverings for the Guru Granth Sahib

sangat Congregation or assembly of Sikhs

sewa Service to others – an essential part of the life of every Sikh

shabads Hymns from the Guru Granth Sahib

Singh Literally, lion. The name is given to every male Sikh, following an instruction from Guru Gobind Singh.

Vand Chhakna Sharing one's time, talents, and earnings with people who are less fortunate

Index

Acknowledgements

The author and publishers thank the following for permission to reproduce photographs:

Circa Photo Library pp 5, 6 (Barrie Searle), 18 bottom (John Smith), 19 top, 24 top (John Smith), 29 (John Smith), 40 (John Smith), 45 (John Smith), 57 (John Smith), 58 (John Smith); Eye Ubiquitous pp 7 left, 17 right (David Cumming), 25 (David Cumming), 50 (Tim Page); Hutchison Library pp 28 left, 31 (Liba Taylor), 32 left, 33, 35 left (N. Durrell McKenna); Christine Osborne Pictures pp 26 left, 34, 35 right, 37, 41 bottom, 53 left, 60, 61; Peter Sanders pp 27, 53 right; TRIP pp 8 (D. Maybury), 10 (H. Rogers), 19 bottom (H. Rogers), 21 (H. Rogers), 23 (G. Fleming), 24 bottom (H. Rogers), 26 right (H. Rogers), 32 right (H. Rogers), 44 (B. Dhanjal), 48 (H. Rogers), 49 (H. Rogers), 51 (H. Rogers), 54 (H. Rogers).

The photographs on pages 7, 9, 13, 30, 36, 38, 39, 41 (top), and 52 are from the author's collection.

The reproductions of paintings on pages 14, 15, 16, 17 left, 18 top, 20, 22, 28 bottom, 46, 55, and 56 are reproduced courtesy of Ramghria Sabha, Southall.

Every reasonable effort has been made to contact copyright owners, but we apologise for any unknown errors or omissions. The list will be corrected, if necessary, in the next reprint.

Illustrations by Gecko Limited pp 4, 13; Tony Morris pp 11, 12, 22, 47, 59.

OXFORD
UNIVERSITY PRESS

Great Clarendon Street, Oxford OX2 6DP

Oxford University Press is a department of the University of Oxford. It furthers the University's objective of excellence in research, scholarship, and education by publishing worldwide in

Oxford New York

Auckland Bangkok Buenos Aires Cape Town Chennai Dar es Salaam Delhi Hong Kong Istanbul Karachi Kolkata Kuala Lumpur Madrid Melbourne Mexico City Mumbai Nairobi São Paulo Shanghai Taipei Tokyo Toronto

Oxford is a registered trade mark of Oxford University Press in the UK and in certain other countries

First published 1998

ISBN 0 19 917255 2

A CIP catalogue record for this book is available from the British Library.

10 9 8 7 6 5 4

Printed in China